Portrait of Leland Case by his niece, Marilyn Sunderman, 1966 hangs in the Case Dakota Art Gallery in the Friends of the Middle Border Museum, Mitchell SD (courtesy of Friends of the Middle Border)

THE MAN
FROM THE HILLS

A Biography of
Leland Davidson Case

By Jarvis Harriman

For the B & G Collection —
Where I learned to write!
for the Sesquicentennial —

Jarvis Harriman
'40
5-1-95

B
CAS

CONTENTS

v

Introduction

by George McGovern

Every human being is a unique individual. But some members of the human family impress us as being especially unique. Leland Case was one of the special people—an unusually creative, original-minded person endowed with a keen intellectual curiosity, a passionate sense of history, and the energy and boldness to press his friends and associates into serving his varied interests and projects.

"Leland was essentially an idea man", observed my brother-in-law, Professor Robert Pennington of Dakota Wesleyan University. "He had more ideas—some good and some not so good—and he pressed them more with vigor, than anyone else."

Bob Pennington as a devoted student of the American West and a director of one of Mr. Case's favorite causes, the Friends of the Middle Border, was in a position to know and appreciate the ideas of Leland Case.

One cannot read this fascinating account of Mr. Case's life without realizing that he was indeed first and foremost a man of ideas.

I came to know Leland Case when I was a student and then later a professor at Dakota Wesleyan. Our love for this Methodist liberal arts college in Mitchell, South Dakota—my hometown—formed an early bond between us. We were also both sons of Methodist minister fathers. We shared a love for history and for the writers and artists of the upper Great Plains that comprised "the Middle Border" where settlers coming west from the East Coast met up with other adventurers coming back from the West Coast gold rush.

Leland's older brother, Francis, was, like me, a Dakota Wesleyan graduate who went on to become a United States Senator. Clinton Anderson, who served New Mexico in the U.S. Senate after graduating from Dakota Wesleyan, comprised the third of Wesleyan's trio in the Senate—a fact well known to Leland that gave him pride and satisfaction as an ardent supporter of Wesleyan and the Middle Border.

Jarvis Harriman has carefully researched the voluminous Case files, as well as those of his principal associates, and has engaged in enough interviews to capture his subject. This book highlights the impact not only of its subject's boyhood in the Black Hills but also of the continuing relationship of this beautiful, scenic treasure in shaping Mr. Case's life. Former Secretary of the Interior Stewart Udall once described the Black Hills as "an island in the sky". Leland Case was deeply inspired and molded by the magic and majesty of South Dakota's Black Hills. The culture of the Sioux Indians, the life-style of the ranchers, miners, timber men and sportsmen helped to feed his soul and his imagination. He collected their stories and observations—as he did the observations of small town editors, preachers and teachers. As the author observes and documents, the Black Hills was to Leland Case "a lifelong love affair".

For a number of years the most passionate idea in Leland's mind was the Middle Border project at Dakota Wesleyan. He envisioned a dynamic cultural center, complete with a library, museum, art gallery, student fellowships and special research projects — all designed to focus on the cultural life, the historical contributions and the unique character of this region so dear to him. The project still is in operation, but from the first was handicapped by meager funding. Leland, longtime Dakota

Wesleyan Dean and President Matthew Smith, Gordon Rollins—the college business manager, Bob Pennington and Leonard Jennewein who directed the program for several years—all of these and others understood and embraced the Middle Border concept. But like many good ideas, this one did not attract the support of those in a position to finance it.

If I were to single out the most successful of Leland Case's ideas, it would be "The Westerners" dealt with in Chapter V of this biography. This concept was born in the mind of Leland and two of his friends in early 1944 during the time he served as an editor of the Rotary Club magazine. It grew out of their involvement with the Friends of the Middle Border, but was an effort to embrace not simply the history and culture of this one region but of the entire American west.

The format and purpose of the Westerners was to stimulate and enlarge interest in the American West by regular meetings, discussions, papers, a newsletter and other publications. The first chapter, or "corral", of the society was formed in Chicago in 1944 and from this quiet beginning the organizations spread to over a hundred chapters in thirteen countries with a membership of 5000 people. When I was a graduate student in history at Northwestern University following service in WWII, I came to treasure, first as a professor, and later as a friend, Ray Allen Billington — one of the nation's most eminent historians of the American frontier. He became involved early on in the Westerners and developed a friendship with Leland Case. Subsequently he was to become the national president of the Westerners. He loved this organization in part because it embraced not only professional historians and academics, but also business people, doctors, lawyers, editors and Americans in every job category.

There can be no doubt that The Westerners have done much to stimulate a genuine interest in the great drama of the American West. We are indebted to Leland Case for the vision, imagination and enthusiasm that made this remarkable organization a reality.

Just to list the subjects covered in this unfolding tale of the ideas and adventures of Leland Case is to gain an appreciation for the fact that this unusual man of South Dakota and America wasted no time. He was a lifelong student, an avid reader, a prolific writer, an editor, teacher and author; a strong and participating leader in the Methodist Church who edited one of its successful magazines; a political ally of his brother Francis; the collector and designer of a valuable western library, to name a few of his activities.

When he was editor of the *Rotarian*, he became incensed at the anti-Rotary jabs of some celebrities including Clarence Darrow, H.L. Mencken, Sinclair Lewis and George Bernard Shaw. He decided that he would disarm these critics by going to see them individually and then inviting each of them to submit an article to the *Rotarian*. His strategy worked perfectly. The critics of Rotary not only published articles in the *Rotarian*, they never again criticized the organization.

Leland Case was an inveterate letter writer. He kept full, up to date files on a large number of correspondents. Whenever he saw an item in the press that might be of interest to one of his friends, he mailed it with an appropriate note. He also maintained a tickler file to make certain that his friends and acquaintances received regular communications from him.

Reading this book will give the reader a lively and informative account of a remarkably impressive man.

Author's Preface

"I'd like you to come along and sit in on a meeting on Wednesday night. It's our Westerners executive committee, and we meet for supper and to handle the affairs of the organization." I had met Leland Case a couple of weeks before, when I was invited to read a paper to the Tucson Corral, number VI in the growing fellowship of Westerners. I had never heard of the outfit or of Leland until that time.

So I went along that Wednesday evening to a modest spot, the Royal Sun Restaurant in downtown Tucson, where they had a private room and a good, down-home off-the-menu supper, and a jovial group it was. "Green River style", according to Case. "Green River" meant it was taken for granted that each one paid his own tab, and this was fine by me. "Green River", I soon found out, was one of a growing series of "instant traditions" that Westerners, under Case's easy leadership style, adopted "at the drop of a Stetson." The group that evening was composed of historians, writers and history buffs, and was quite varied in make-up and interests.

After the meeting Leland said to me, "You can see what we need is a firm but friendly hand to keep us moving." I said yes, I could see that. "I want you to be our meeting chairman", Case continued, "so that we can get things done instead of going around in circles." I said "But I don't know anything about Westerners." He said "You will. You'll get the hang of it."

Why I agreed to this odd arrangement I still don't know, but I said OK, when's the next meeting. A few weeks later I saw the letterhead of Westerners International. Under the name of the president, Erl Ellis (of Denver) it said "Vice-President:

Jarvis Harriman." That was in 1974. Thirteen years later I stepped down from the offices of Executive Vice-President and then Chairman of the Board. I had done it for Leland Case.

To say that Leland was an interesting man to work with would be an understatement. His mind was away ahead of the rest of us. This is to say that he had put in a lot of thought over many years, on the character and the growth possibilities of The Westerners, and had done far more thinking about it than any of the rest of us. I think, too, that Leland knew he was an irritant a lot of the time, but he accepted that as the price of getting things done. Not many of us–certainly not I—had any real idea of the realms that this man's mind and experience dwelt in. I began to catch glimpses of this as I researched through the hundred-plus file boxes of the contents of his study in preparing to write of his life.

Because of the quality and outreach of Leland's life, and the multitude of personalities and experiences in which he was involved, the work of creating this book has been one of the richest chapters in my seventy-odd years.

Leland Case lived in an era that bridged so many things. The automobile, the airplane, women's suffrage and the coming of meaningful participation of women in world affairs, nuclear power, communications, the civil rights movement, the computer—the changes that took place in his active lifetime were enormous. He kept up with them. The changes in his own industry of journalism, just the processes of printing, for example, he rode with eagerly. And look at his use of words, perhaps his basic stock-in-trade. Look at the inventiveness of his written language.

Leland Case's place in history will probably be defined in two subject categories—Magazine Journalism in the Twentieth Century, and the Influence on Modern Times of the Study of Western American History.

As this book illustrates, Leland took to things so naturally, moved onto a larger stage with no effort. Perhaps he was one of the men who <u>make</u> times. He was not a major world—or national—figure. But surely he was one of the doers, the dreamers who step forward to turn dreams into reality—who embody the best of the "American spirit" and make our country a better, more richly endowed place. And when you get right down to it, the selflessness of most of it is astounding.

Jarvis Harriman
Tucson, Arizona

CHAPTER I
The Boy from the Black Hills

The train rattled and chuffed its way west across the prairie. It was a fall day—cool, Indian summer style—but the coach windows were open for air, in spite of the soot and cinders. The youngster leaning out in order not to miss anything wore a little felt hat pulled down to his ears. His mother wondered when it would blow off. They were going "Out West"—"Indian Country"—where adventure lurked behind every blade of grass.

The family had been travelling for two days on the Northwestern Railroad—departure from Marathon, Iowa; destination Sturgis, South Dakota. The year was 1909, and Mary Ellen Grannis Case was shepherding her five young ones as they journeyed out to join her husband Herbert. Herbert Llywellyn Case, minister of the gospel, was answering a call to the Black Hills for the Methodist Episcopal Church.

Herbert and Mary had married at her father's farm in Vernon, Minnesota, but he was from Iowa. Because of his ministry they had moved every couple of years. The five children were born in five different towns in Iowa: Joyce, the eldest, in 1895, in Renwick; Francis, 1896, in Everly; Leland, 1900, in Wesley; Caroline, 1903, in Swaledale; and Esther, 1907, in Marathon.

When Herbert accepted the call to South Dakota, he sold his fast horse for $125 and used it to pay for his railway tickets. They were for an "emigrant car," a boxcar that the railroad made available at special rates to people moving into the new territories, and coach tickets for his wife and children to follow him. Then everything he and Mary felt was worth moving, he loaded into the boxcar: two young horses, Dolly and Queen;

1

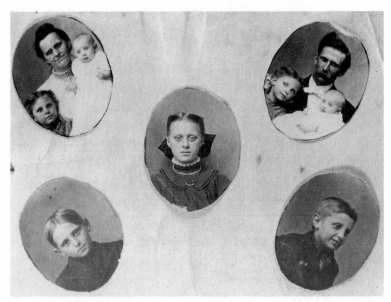

The Case family about 1910—(upper left) Mary Grannis Case with Carol and Esther, (center) Joyce, (upper right) Herbert Llywellyn Case with Carol and Esther, (lower left) Francis, (lower right) Leland

their cow and some chickens; farm and shop tools; bedding, clothes, and kitchen utensils; their golden oak bedroom set and their new Epworth piano, a mahogany beauty that Joyce was learning to play. Then he climbed in himself. Off he went to western South Dakota to begin his ministry and to prepare for the rest of his family.

Neighbors in Marathon packed a basket for the family because they knew it cost too much to feed five missionaries' children on the train. The food didn't last long. The journey, 600 miles, took two days, and by the second day Mrs. Case was cutting apples into very small slices to make them go farther. Carol and Esther had to be content with smaller portions because they were the youngest.

The Boy from the Black Hills

Kerosene lights stayed on in the car all night, but the children managed to sleep some. The rest of the time they—especially Francis and Leland—were craning out the windows to see the West. Mother had her back to the boys, but her eye caught a flash as Leland's hat blew off, and she made a grab for it. The second time it blew off she was engrossed in conversation with her daughters and missed it. The hat sailed by and down under the wheels of the train. Mother solved the problem of the dust and grime by tying knots in the four corners of one of her husband's large handkerchiefs and pulling that over her younger son's head to try and keep him clean.

Just before they were to arrive, the two smallest girls went to the bathroom at the end of the car. Suddenly the door opened and the conductor yelled "Scooptown! Scooptown!" The little girls, terrified, ran back to Mama—"Oh, Mama, we've missed Sturgis!" until someone explained that Scooptown was what Sturgis was called by most everyone around those parts. The troops at nearby Fort Meade had thought up the name because they felt the local merchants managed to scoop up most of their money on paydays.

It was dusk when they pulled into the station. There was their father, handsome and welcoming. He had brought the baby carriage from the parsonage to carry their things because his horses were young and unused to the likes of steam engines, and he didn't want to risk a runaway. So they piled things into the carriage and put baby Esther on top. With Joyce making sure she didn't fall out, the family trudged down the boardwalk and through the evening light to their new home.

Thus began the Case family's life in the Black Hills, which, especially for Leland Davidson Case, was to be a lifelong love affair.

The Case family on their claim north of Bear Butte in 1910—left to right: Carol, Francis, Joyce standing behind Mrs. Case, Esther beside Mrs. Case's knee, Leland with Peggy, and The Rev. Mr. Case. Photographer's carriage in right background.

To the youngsters the move was exciting. To Herbert and Mary, though they did it gladly, it meant a lot of work. When Herbert had arrived in Sturgis he had found the town over-flowing with homesteaders. The former pastor was still living in the parsonage. Mr. Case could not find a room nor even hire a chair in the hotel lobby. He went back to the boxcar and slept in the bed his farmer friends in Marathon had fixed up for him. He had to use a ladder to climb in and out of the car. The first sermon Herbert preached in Sturgis before his family got there started like this: "Most charges wish their pastor to come into the pulpit looking as if he had stepped out of a bandbox, but, unable to hire a room or even a chair, I come out of a boxcar."

A few days later a portion of the church ceiling fell around Herbert's shoulders, and for several days he and some of the

4

men worked to replace it with a metal one. Then he put a new galvanized roof on the parsonage, the former minister having finally departed. Mr. Case was always working to fix things up and make them better—a man handy with his hands.

In those days, Carol tagged around after her brother Leland much of the time. They were at the adventurous ages of six and nine, respectively. They found the parsonage exciting. Upstairs were two bedrooms and then space for a couple of more, but it was unfinished, with a few boards scattered on the floor joists. They went exploring up there one day, looking for buried treasure. Put back inside a dark space they found an old baking powder can. When they pried off the lid, it held a lot of pennies. To them this was wealth!

Francis and Leland had one of the upstairs bedrooms, and Joyce and Carol the other. Dad and Mother had the "best" bedroom downstairs, with baby Esther, and their golden oak furniture. Mother had a sewing room. Her brand new White Family Rotary sewing machine with two secret drawers, a sewing table with ruling along the front edge, a long mirror trimmed with gold, and even the old cradle that Grandpa Grannis had made for her when she was born were its furnishings.

The sewing room was important because the family got most of their clothes out of missionary barrels. Most of the contents came as "seconds" from Sears and Roebuck, as well as "hand-me-downs" that folks back east sent to the mission fields. Mother became an expert at reworking dresses and blouses for the girls, shirts and pants for the boys, underwear and pajamas for them all—just about everything the family needed. Mary Grannis had been her family's eldest, and had grown up a confident, self-reliant young woman who rode horses, plowed the fields, led her sisters and brother and was

5

Leland Case, aged about eleven, with the porcupine he killed at "the claim".
Leland was posed with this 22-calibre rifle, although he knew he had killed the
porcupine with a rock. Drawing from a lost photograph, made by Leland's friend
Paul A. Rossi.

the pride of her parents. Now all of that ability was directed to the care of her husband and of her own brood.

Leland had a puppy, a Scottish sheep dog that he named Peggy. Boy and dog became fast friends, growing up together— Leland said later that he was more fond of Peggy than of anyone else in the family. That was probably true in a sense, but the family lasted longer than Peggy did.

The parsonage had at least one distinguished visitor that the children never forgot. Carrie A. Nation, the nationally-known prohibitionist, came to town on her crusade against what she called The "Demon Rum." Leland and Carol followed Dad and Mrs. Nation downtown to a saloon, where she wished to demonstrate her protest. Mr. Case was a thoughtful man, so he had warned the saloon keeper earlier. When Carrie came in, the proprietor announced that they were just closing up and coming to the church to hear her talk. Off they went with her, closing the place tight as they left for Divine Service, thereby avoiding the destruction of the place by her well-known hatchet, which the powerful woman kept in a secret pocket in her voluminous skirt. She had destroyed many a bar and saloon in other towns.

Those were still relatively lawless days when the Reverend Mr. Case had to be ready for anything. Years later Leland still kept in his study in Tucson the brass knuckles that his father had carried in his pocket for emergencies.

In coming to the Black Hills, Mr. Case, with his energy and his humanity, so appealed to people that they were travelling to church from great distances, sometimes 75 and 100 miles. In response to this he picked two schoolhouses, located in outlying places, in which to hold additional services.

After a year in Sturgis, Herbert moved his family to be more strategically located for his work in the whole area. He chose a spot 10 miles out of town and a mile north of Bear Butte. He picked up a "relinquishment," a claim that someone had not been able to "prove up" on (acquire permanent title to from the government by making improvements to it within the time allowed). He acquired a small two-room house not too far away and moved it to the new site with the help of his friends.

The site they picked for their house was an historic one. Generations of Indians had raised their tipis on that spot, gathering there for ceremonies at Bear Butte, as they had for centuries. The great meeting of 1857 had taken place there when Crazy Horse had joined his father in pledging to drive the White Man out of the Hills country forever. Where they had camped you could still see tipi rings, circles of stones that had been gathered to hold down the coverings of their lodges. The tipi rings were the source of much of the material the men gathered for a foundation for the Cases' home.

The house was really quite substantial, for a claim structure. It was sheathed in rusty tin embossed to look like brick. There were two rooms. One room was divided by a curtain. The parents took one half for their bedroom and the girls, the other. The boys slept on a couch in the second room where the piano and the rest of their simple furnishings were. Their golden oak bedroom set and some of their best things they left in the parsonage in Sturgis, which they still maintained.

There was a well on the claim, but the alkali water took some getting used to. Often they took their spring wagon and some clean milk cans and went off to the neighbors' for sweet water. Sometimes good water was scarce, and they'd use the same potful to boil their meal and then to make the coffee.

They dug another well, but that turned out to be dry; Dad lined it with stones so they could store butter and vegetables in the cool down there. They built a cowshed; the hayloft could be approached by wagon on the up-hill side, and the cow was quartered below.

Life became full of new things for the children. Everyone had chores to do. Francis helped with the plowing. Joyce and the girls helped with cooking and with keeping the little house neat. Leland didn't like milking the cow much or the smell of her quarters in the shed, but he'd cut a switch for Carol, and she'd keep the flies off both him and the cow while he milked and told her stories. That's the way the milking was done. Dad also set Leland to clearing a fire break around the buildings with the plow—he knew the terror of a prairie fire in those parts. Twice around with the plow made a six-foot swath.

Leland developed a line of traps for jackrabbits. They were good eating. He and Carol and Peggy would roam out across the claim, winter and summer, checking the traps. Leland did this with care, so the rabbits he caught would be in good condition when he got them home for the table.

He found some old round cheese boxes, and he used some of them to build a pigeon house up on the shed roof. Francis and Leland had earned a BB gun, a Daisy Air Rifle, by selling subscriptions to the magazine *Youth Companion.* They would shoot at the pigeons and then have meat for supper. They learned to poke around by the creek with a length of pipe and pin a frog to the ground. Then they would take him home for fried frog's legs. They also fished in the creek.

Always when Leland and Carol were out he would tell her stories—about going out West, finding treasure, and doing adventurous things.

9

It was the boys' job to get the chickens ready for the pot when that was the menu. Usually they would select the chicken, take it out in the yard and swing it until it was dizzy enough to be dealt with, and then chop its head off. This particular time they decided they'd shoot it with their gun. The swinging hadn't quite immobilized the chicken the first time, so Leland reached for it to swing it again, just as Francis pulled the trigger. The BB hit him right in the lower lip and lodged there.

Their father, who had always wanted to be a doctor, sent for the bottle of Listerine on the kitchen shelf, got the BB out with a toothpick and cleaned the wound with the antiseptic. Otherwise the family would have had to hitch up the wagon and dash 10 miles to Sturgis to the doctor—the fear of lockjaw was very real to them.

But Dad was angry, too; so angry that he demanded the air rifle, and the boys never saw it again. Forty years later Leland was poking around the foundation of the house, which was long gone, and found the rusting spring and part of the barrel of the rifle, which Dad must have slipped into a hole under the flooring and left there.

There were still signs around Bear Butte of the great herds of buffalo that had been almost obliterated from this prairie land. One weathered buffalo skull they found Leland kept— and years later in Tucson it hung in his office, a reminder of those early days.

It wasn't all work. The boys played baseball over at Ezra Bovee's, their nearest neighbors. There was plenty of "hide and seek", and "fox and geese" on the sparse-covered ground. In the winter they made snowmen in the snow. One source of delight was the dump at Fort Meade, the army post located between Bear Butte and Sturgis that had been founded during the Indian Wars. Families leaving when their tour of duty was up would deposit all kinds of treasures there for a child to find.

Out on the claim there was a big corner post at the entrance. At the post dump they found a discarded uniform—Spanish American War. They brought it home and nailed it onto the post, and topped it with an old hat. From then on the entrance post was known as "Old Man." They went to the dump with Dad one day; he found a big wheel from a washing machine, and a child's broken rocking chair, and some chunks of wood. He used them as parts to make a merry-go-round. One child would sit on it, and another would walk around and around. That was how they gave each other rides.

Fort Meade also was where they got firewood. Mr. Case got a permit from the adjutant to take deadfalls in the woods of the military reservation. That kept the fires going in winter and provided for the cooking all year round. Hot water for baths was heated in a big tub on a stove they had also found at the dump.

In the evenings they played carroms, snapping rings across a board that had a pocket in the end—Mother liked that, and when the pocket wore out, she crocheted another one. And checkers and dominos. And jigsaw puzzles made from pictures torn from old magazines and glued onto thin wood, which they cut into pieces. And they sang. Joyce went every two weeks into town to the Sisters at St. Martin's Academy for piano lessons, and at home she loved to play. They would sing hymns, and the tunes of the day, such as "Hello Central, Give Me Heaven, for My Momma's There".

The parents loved to sing. Sometimes for church socials they would dress up, and Joyce would accompany them on the piano. Sometimes they all sang parts and rounds, while the

11

kerosene lamps burned brightly. There was never a black lamp chimney because they used old paper to clean them.

There was labor trouble that year at the Homestake Mine over in Lead, some 25 miles away. The company mounted a big searchlight on top of the Eliason hoist, and they played it over the area, looking for troublemakers. The Case children would climb up on the roof of the house at the claim and watch the beam of the searchlight. They'd pop popcorn on the stove and take it up with them. They waited there trying to guess when the searchlight would swing back toward them again.

The children played with the Bovees, and sometimes they'd go to town together. On the Fourth of July Mr. Bovee loaded them all into his big wagon and they went in to see the fireworks. After the show Mr. Bovee took them all over to the hamburger wagon and ordered big ones for everybody—and another one if anyone could eat it. This was a special treat because, on their own, Dad and Mother would have had to order one for each two of them, and they'd have to share.

Not all the neighbors were like the Bovees. One neighbor man saw that the Cases had a second dog, Carlo, a black and white, in addition to Peggy. He talked to Papa about Carlo, because his son didn't have a dog, he said. So they parted with Carlo for the sake of the boy. Then one day Leland and Carol and Amos Bovee were out poking around near Bear Butte. There was an old barn there, on the edge of the neighbor's claim. They pushed the door open on its creaky hinges and peered in. There was Carlo's hide, stretched out on the wall to dry. And a few weeks later they spotted the neighbor man wearing a pair of black and white mittens!

Leland had one hard lesson to learn with Peggy. "We used to go on Sundays to church," Leland recalled, "at what was

12

called the May Schoolhouse, east of Bear Butte. (This was one of the additional locations where Mr. Case was holding services to better serve his people.) One Sunday when we came home there was evidence that Peggy had eaten a chicken. This happened two Sundays in a row and the family served an ultimatum that this would stop or Peggy would go. Well, I confided the matter to Peggy and the next Sunday there was nothing. But the second Sunday following we came home and here was evidence that I found over in a gulch a little ways from the house that she had eaten another chicken.

"Well, this was a pretty desperate situation. I took Peggy over to the scene of the crime. She knew that she had done wrong, I mean she did not want to go with me, but I forced her to go and I would rub her nose into the half devoured wings or whatever. Although I myself would have rather been horsewhipped, I had a stick and I beat her and then I would rub her nose in it and beat her again. She whined and howled, and it was pitiful. This went on for quite a while, but from that moment on she never touched a chicken. In fact, she used to seem to enjoy letting the little ones jump all over her."

Mr. Case got an itinerant photographer to come out to the claim in his buggy one day, and the whole family lined up for a picture—Momma in the middle in her chair; Esther by her knee with her favorite doll; Joyce, the tallest, behind her; Carol with her doll, beside Francis; Leland with the dog Peggy at his side; and Dad in his jacket and tie.

Later someone took a picture of Leland by the shed. He was standing with a gun in his hand and a porcupine he had bagged placed on a barrel beside him. They insisted on the gun because it made a good picture, but he never felt comfortable about it because he knew he had killed the porcupine with a rock.

13

The family had the spring wagon for hauling things and they had a buggy. Mr. Case usually drove his circuit with the buggy. The roads—or lack of them—are what made his trips hard. Covering his territory took a lot out of him, even though he was a strong man. Often he was away, and Mary was there on the claim with the children, with her bright spirit and inventive mind. She helped with lessons. They all read a lot, and Leland taught Carol at such an early age, she could hardly remember a time when she did not read.

They "proved up" on 120 acres during that year. That land was to stand them in good stead a bit later.

The year was a bad one for Sturgis and for Mr. Case's congregation. The crops failed, the bank failed, and times were hard. Mr. Case distributed 60 barrels of clothing that year to needy Methodist families, all gifts from people who were better off. Altogether he helped over 500 individuals who needed support.

The scarcity of good water and the paucity of decent roads were two things that remained in the memory of Francis Case his whole life. Years later as a member of Congress, water and roads were two of his major interests, and his record in the House and the Senate for 26 years proves it.

These days of few resources stayed with the family forever. They didn't know they were poor! They felt sorry for other people who had less than they had. They ate a lot of bread and milk, but that was good. They never seemed to quarrel. They were very happy, and they loved each other.

In 1912 Herbert Case accepted an additional assignment. He became Superintendent of the Cheyenne River District of the Dakota Conference of the Methodist Church. This district covered even more territory—from the Black Hills to the Missouri River.

14

Herbert and Mary wanted their children to have the best possible education, so they moved the family to Mitchell, some 70 miles east of the Missouri. Herbert stayed behind. His headquarters were at Philip, and he rode the train, rode horseback, hitched rides, and walked to cover that immense West River territory. He established little Methodist churches throughout. It was hard, pioneering work.

For the family, Mitchell was a change from the prairie home near Bear Butte. It was a town. On Pennington Avenue they rented a house that had a big garden and room to raise chickens. The older children went to Dakota Wesleyan Academy, which was operated by Dakota Wesleyan University in Mitchell, as so many smaller-town colleges did in those days.

Leland found several new ways to help with the family finances. He would take a basket and go to the Turner Creamery, down near the railroad tracks, to get cottage cheese. He'd take Carol with him, and they would sell the cheese from door to door. He figured Carol brought him more customers. The family didn't like the cottage cheese from the creamery as well as what they made at home—the creamery made it with pasteurized milk, and they could taste the difference—but they could get more and sell more that way. Leland had a list of regular customers, as well as ones he encountered along the way, and if there were any left he'd bring it home.

The two of them also sold chickens. He and Carol would help Mother clean and dress them. Then off they'd go, selling chickens for 50 cents apiece. Some of their customers lived so far out that they'd take the one-seater buggy. A woman on the other side of town had a standing order with them for two fryers every Thursday. Once when they went to her house, Carol was left outside holding the horse's reins while Leland went in.

15

When people he delivered to offered him cookies, he would cram them into his pockets so he'd have some for Carol. This time the woman offered him cake with frosting. He hesitated over how to handle this. The woman looked out the window, saw Carol in the buggy and realized what the predicament was. So she insisted he bring Carol in to enjoy the treat. Leland tied the horse to the hitching post and brought his sister in to have cake with him.

They moved to a big house on South Edmunds Street that had a prairie schooner porch on the second floor. There wasn't another house like that one in town. Now they had a smaller yard without room for so much enterprise. Mary took in two young Englishmen as boarders. They were studying for the ministry. She also took a girl in about Joyce's age, who shared a room with Joyce and was to help Mother by doing some of the housework.

What with schooling and Bible reading, the children were learning a lot. Leland liked to show Carol off. He'd prompt her to recite a verse of scripture. Then he'd say, "Now she'll do it backwards." So Carol would turn around and recite it again with her back to her audience.

During much of the year in Mitchell, Mr. Case was away from home, and Mary took care of the family by herself.

In 1913 Mr. Case took a church in Hot Springs, and back to the Black Hills they went. Herbert and Mary sold the claim near Bear Butte and used the proceeds to buy a home for Herbert's parents, who moved from Iowa to be near them. Now there were grandparents nearby to add another dimension to the childrens' lives.

Leland joined the Boy Scouts. There were knots to be learned, semaphore and Morse code with flags, and first aid.

They went swimming at several of the establishments in town, where warm water from the springs had drawn people over the centuries. Leland taught Carol to swim. At Mammoth Plunge or Evans or Minnekahta Plunge they'd spend hours perfecting floating, swimming underwater, or picking up stones from the bottom. Leland sold Fuller Brush products door-to-door and mowed the lawn at the house of a prominent family for 10 cents an hour, plus cookies—and the lady really knew how to bake cookies.

Leland discovered theater. He loved acting, directing, and putting on plays in school. They also would go to band concerts at the Battle Mountain Sanitarium.

Someone gave the family a duck for a holiday gift. Leland became quite fond of it and named it Suzie. He even built a little pen for it outside. He would go out and sit on the buggy seat and quack at Suzie and she would quack back at him. A girl named Rose who came from Oelrichs worked for the family, and she often teased Leland about his duck. When Suzie eventually grew old, Mr. Case killed and dressed her for dinner, and they had roast duck. This was one meal when Leland didn't eat meat. After dinner, he carefully took the tail bone, cleaned it and let it dry for a couple of days, and then wrapped it in tissue paper. He mailed it to Rose, who was back home by this time. The card he enclosed read, "The End of Suzie."

Leland and a friend built a boat. They floated it down Fall River, pulled it back upstream with a rope and floated down again. They had to keep caulking it to keep it afloat, but it was handy to drift along and get frogs with a hook baited with a red piece of cloth. Leland would dress them—some pretty good size, and the legs would be great eating.

Sometimes Dad took the children and their friends out in the wagon to a place where they could camp.

Francis graduated from Hot Springs High School and went on to study at Dakota Wesleyan University in Mitchell. The family then moved to Spearfish for a year. There was no proper high school for Leland there, so he attended classes at Spearfish Normal, the teachers' college in that part of the state. He was quite proud of the fact that he had done well in a college setting.

In 1917 Herbert Case took on a different kind of work, as financial agent for the Deaconess Hospital at Rapid City (now known as the Bennett-Clarkson Hospital), which principally meant he was raising money for the institution. He learned to drive the hospital's old Model T runabout to facilitate his work.

Leland attended Rapid City High School. He did well in English composition and got high marks for his writing. He reported on high school news for the *Rapid City Daily Journal*, which seems to have been his first taste of the craft that thereafter became the heart of his professional life. He kept up his interest in theater. The family recalls his part in a play called *The Gods of the Mountain*. He painted scenery for it as well as acting in it. He was dressed in rags and tatters. In the plot the townspeople were supposed to sic their dogs on him. When they did so, the dogs went up and licked his hands.

Poetry began to appear in his school work. Consider the following verse for a 17-year-old and what it reveals of adolescence and a maturing boy:

While Wranglin on the Range
I see her face in my campfire,
Her eyes shine in the sky.

18

The Boy from the Black Hills

Her form is in the misty clouds -
Her presence ever nigh.

The fire commands me to be pure,
The stars look down on me.
The clouds reveal their lining,
...And, I am kept for her and thee.

And the following, written as America was getting into the first world war:

I Follow

I hear the tread of tramping feet,
I hear the bugle call.
The creaking leather — groaning guns,
I hear, I feel it all.

I see, I hear, I feel, I know,
For, since the world began
Men have followed men to war,
I know — I am a man.

Yes, the boys are marching by,
They too have heard that call,
And answered, true, as men will do
— I too shall give my all.

Francis graduated from Dakota Wesleyan in the spring of 1918 and came back to the Case home at Rapid City. The nation was at war with Germany. Francis' forebears had served in the American Revolution and the Civil War, and he was determined to enlist in the armed forces rather than waiting for the draft. He decided on the Marine Corps, and that meant going to Denver. He was to catch the train down the line near Hermosa, 25 miles or so south of Rapid City.

THE MAN FROM THE HILLS

Mary Case suggested that Leland drive his brother to Hermosa in the little old family Ford. The boys called it "Wounded Knee" because they were always having trouble with it. To get to Hermosa there were no graded roads, really, and the washes often were sinks of "blue gumbo" that would accumulate under the fenders and stop the car. Halfway through one such wash, the car groaned to a stop.

"It was one of the worst moments in my life," Leland recalled. "I was driving, and here was my brother going off to war. If I didn't get him to Hermosa in time, he would miss the train and then he would be drafted and that would be ignominy without end for the family. I insisted that he stay in the car while I do the dirty work. I rolled in the mud so much that day, a day later my trousers would stand by themselves in the corner.

"Along after midnight we pulled out of the mess and rolled along toward this little town. Out about two miles "Wounded Knee" couldn't make it up the hill. There was nothing to do but to leave the car by the side of the road and walk in and try to get a little sleep at a hotel. I bid Francis goodbye the next morning. Then I went out to try to get the car going. In those days every kid could adjust a Ford carburetor, and I adjusted ours. I backed up, steamed up that hill, throttle open, and I stalled again. Then an idea began to glimmer. The gas tank was under the seat and there was only gravity flow. So I turned "Wounded Knee" around and backed up the hill like a sky rocket!"

CHAPTER II
The Boy Becomes a Man of the World

Leland graduated from Rapid City High School in the spring of 1918. That summer he enlisted in the Student Army Training Corps. They were quartered in filthy old chicken houses, and the boys had to clean them out. His family felt afterwards that this was the start of Leland's lung trouble, which became such a problem 20 years later.

Leland enrolled that fall in Dakota Wesleyan University, which had become familiar to him during the year they had lived in Mitchell. College life was an expansive time for Leland.

It was a busy time—a full academic load, football practice, and military drill. During horseplay around the dormitory, a folding cot collapsed, catching Leland's big toe. On the parade ground the next day he couldn't keep up with the formation but Leland refused to quit. Chagrined and lagging behind, the lone figure drew applause from the sidelines.

Involved in a wrestling match with a friend one day, Leland grew exhausted and was ready to quit, but for some impulsive reason he held on a bit longer. To his surprise his opponent, evidently tired out too, gave in—so the decision went to Leland.

A classmate recalls that Leland was full of ginger and liked to tease people. A group of students preparing for divinity studies was called the Oxford Club. To Leland and his friends, the members seemed to trade on their piety. "We got a bit fed up, me and my gang," he said later, "with the favors shown by the faculty to the Oxford Club, composed of preacher-bent students who (it seemed to us) would "pray" rather than "study" their way through exams. We organized secretly—so our notice read—a rival Cambridge Club. It was to meet at midnight

21

in the 'dome shaped shrine,' otherwise known as the observatory. Our motto was 'Work to beat the Devil!'"

The local gathering spot was the Campus Cafe. One day, Leland's friend Robert Eri Wood brought along some carbon disulfide from the chemistry lab, which they smeared on the back of the cafe's cat. The cat chased wildly all over the room and up and over the tables until the boys opened the door so it could get out. It disappeared and was never seen again. Miss Ketchum, the cook, decided Leland was the perpetrator and never did forgive him for it.

They sang all the popular songs and invented their own words. Nicknames were popular. Leland was "Andrea del Sarto," Renaissance artist, and Wood was "Rabbi Ben Ezra," one of the great Talmudic scholars of the pre-Christian era.

Leland also served as a reporter for *The Mitchell Gazette*, covering activities of the college campus. *The Gazette* wrote in a letter of reference, "He handled his work in an excellent fashion. I would be glad to recommend him for similar work."

One of Leland's short English papers at DWU was titled

"The Cheyenne:"
"Dirty yellow with silt pilfered from innumerable plains and arroyos, the waters of the Cheyenne gnawed unceasingly at the great inclined plane of crumbling, blue shale, once the heart of the hill. Guileful ripples sparkled in the sun furnace, siren-like, trying to lure my feet to the treacherous half-submerged islands of sand where bleached prongs of driftwood stood like guide posts to hell, stark and ghastly. Upstream stretched a long meandering ribbon of bleak sand and wracked, scrubby cottonwoods; downstream rolled a panorama of desolateness, but the Cheyenne, unheeding, maliciously scurried southward to the grey unknown, the sinister Badlands."

22

This paper was marked "A."

Romance also played its part; consider this poem:

"Dear Deby"
The past has gone, but has left behind
The thoughts that now fill my heart,
The sweetest of all as they come to my mind
Breathe a fragrance of what thou are;(sic)
The creek murmurs softly as it flows,
The birds sweetly sing near by
The wild flowers perfume the soft wind that blows...

Unfinished!

After his second year at Dakota Weslyan, Leland moved on to Macalester College in St. Paul, Minnesota. At Dakota Wesleyan he felt that he was in the shadow of his brother Francis. Francis had distinguished himself as an orator of national calibre and as a debater, had played football, worked on the school newspaper, and was a brilliant student. Leland found his brother's reputation a bit heavy to carry. Family changes made the move to Macalester a sensible one. His family had left the Black Hills for Mankato, south of St. Paul, to be near Mary's mother and father, the Samuel Grannises.

Leland competed for a Rhodes Scholarship, which offered the opportunity to study at Oxford University in England, but narrowly missed being chosen. He wrote to the two men who had been chosen, wishing them the best of luck, and to the selection committee asking for their comments in order to learn from the experience.

During all his college years, Leland supported himself and paid his own way. He had that rare mixture of self-confidence and a reticence about boasting, but he remembered a Chatauqua

23

lecturer admonishing his audience: "He who tooteth not his own horn, the same shall remain untooted."

While studying at Macalester, Leland also found time to take some courses in history at the University of Minnesota. He entered the Masonic order, being raised in Macalester Lodge #290. A few years later he resigned from the Lodge because his professional career took prodigious amounts of time and energy and his life had become full to overflowing. He was not associated with Masonry again until quite a bit later in life.

Leland received his Bachelor of Arts degree at Macalester in 1922. That same year his grandmother, Armenia Lewis Grannis, died in Mankato. His grandfather Samuel Grannis moved to St. Cloud, northwest of St. Paul, to combine households with his daughter, Leland's aunt Edith, and her fellow librarian friend Mamie Martin. These two unmarried ladies, both "Aunties" to Leland and his brother and sisters, were to play a part in Leland's life for many years. After retirement, they both moved to Tucson, where they were close to Leland and his wife until they died in the 1970s.

After graduation, Leland secured a job teaching at the St. Cloud Technical High School. He turned out to be a good teacher, and his lively nature seemed to win the loyalty and attention of his students. He served as advisor to *The Tech*, the school's newspaper. He had a room in the home of his aunties and grandfather.

One evening at the supper table Leland mentioned that a barnstorming pilot had flown into town and offered a circle tour over the city for three dollars. "As casually as possible," Leland recalled, "I announced that tomorrow I would fly with him — then awaited protests. Grandpa tugged at his beard. 'Are many going up?' he finally asked. I assured him that the pilot was doing well and hadn't had a mishap. 'Then I'll fly too,' he said in his that's-all- there-is-to-it way.

"I gulped and Aunt Edith started to sputter 'But Daddy!' 'You see,' he went on, 'when I was a boy back in New Hampshire I rode the first train of cars we had there. Here in Minnesota I courted your Grandma in an ox-cart — and later bought the nicest new buggy in Vernon Center. Now we have an automobile. Leland, I'm 83 years old and if I'm going to fly before I die, I'd better go with you tomorrow.'

"Fly he did. I vividly recall the grin of gratification spreading over his face as he passed the headgear to me for my turn aloft. It was a great day for both of us, and we said so to the pilot. He was a young Swede fellow, name of Lindbergh. How could I possibly know that five years later in France, I, then a reporter for the *Paris Herald*, would be interviewing him about a hop he had completed the day before across the Atlantic."

After a year of teaching at St. Cloud, Leland joined his brother in Rapid City, for the summer. Back to the Black Hills! Francis and a friend had purchased a quarter-interest in the *Rapid City Journal*. Leland worked as a writer and reporter.

John Stanley, owner of the *Lead Daily Call*, said to Leland, "Come on over and be my city editor." So he took the job. The paper had a staff of two—a female linotype operator who also wrote the social columns and Leland who did most of the reporting. He took a couple of rooms and a small bathroom on the first floor of a rooming house.

After he settled in, his sister Carol visited him for a few days. She discovered how he was training himself to be a competent newspaperman. In the bathroom, he had taken huge sheets of newsprint and fastened them with clamps to the wall on each side of the handbasin. On the left side was a column headed "Date"—then "People I have met" and "What we talked about." On the right side the sheets were headed "New Words," "Pronounciations," "Meanings and How Used." She said years later, "I've always thought that's how Leland became friends with so many and could call them by name. He trained himself to remember."

In the summer of 1924 the governor of South Dakota, W. H. McMaster, declared his candidacy for the United States Senate. His opponent was Ulysseys S. Grant Cherry, a corporation lawyer who had the support of the Homestake Mine, the Ku Klux Klan, Standard Oil, International Harvester, and the railroads—a true assortment of interests. *The Lead Call* took up the cause of McMaster, and sent Leland with him on the campaign trail. John Stanley ran the paper while Leland was away. The campaign was fought largely on whether "big business" should control the state. Leland filed dispatches to *The Call* from Deadwood, Rapid City, Sioux Falls, Yankton, Mitchell, and Aberdeen, and acted as McMasters' press aid. McMaster won the election.

Leland stayed with the *Daily Call* for nearly two years. It was hard, steady work. Still, he found time to keep up his hereditary interest in the Methodist Church, and to be president of the church Men's Club. He also found time to explore some of the historic sites and the background of tales told by the old-timers. Leland discovered that people believed young fellows like he were not supposed to have an interest in history—that was the preserve of the old fogeys around the place. But interested he was, and his files began to grow with material on the Black Hills and their history.

Two of his heroes were Jedediah Strong Smith, the first white man to go overland through the Dakotas, across the

Rockies, and to California; and Preacher Henry Weston Smith, who was murdered near Deadwood on his way to hold a church service. His interest in these men endured to the end of his life. Then there were all the usual characters—Wild Bill Hickok and Calamity Jane being the Black Hills' most widely known.

Leland's appreciation of the Black Hills matured in those years. They were "Paha Sapa"to the Sioux translated literally "Hills Black." Roughly 125 miles north to south and 50 miles across, granite outcroppings were set about with pine, and cedar, and juniper; peaks as high as 7200 feet; vales of rich grass; and bear, deer, birds, and small game.

Leland traveled a lot—to the northeast edge where his family had lived in Sturgis and Bear Butte, with Spearfish and Belle Fourche to the west and north. He journeyed from Sturgis into the Hills proper, to Lead and Deadwood—with winding valleys and canyons, the Homestake Mine, and deeper still to Keystone and Mt. Rushmore; south to Hill City, Custer, and Custer State Park, and Hot Springs at the southern edge; on the east, Rapid City, fast growing to be the key commercial center. On their western slopes, the Black Hills spilled over into Wyoming. It was a magic area, unique in all the West.

Those months—first at the *Journal* and then the *Call*, were Leland's basic training in journalism. Out of this experience he emerged a journeyman newspaperman with ink under his fingernails. If the aides posted in his bathroom were sharpening his faculties, the day-by-day work at the paper was honing his skills in reporting, writing, editing and producing a newspaper.

Then one day while writing one of those seasonal stories— about the weather or something—he had occasion to look back through his file of the previous year. He found he had written the same story almost word for word. He went to Mr. Stanley, the owner, and told him he was resigning. "Why's that?," the boss asked. "Because I'm getting into a rut." Stanley protested that he wanted to sell Leland the paper on terms he could pay off by working. Leland stuck to his decision, and left the *Lead Call* to become a better journalist. He went to Chicago to attend the new Medill School of Journalism at Northwestern University.

Studying journalism in Chicago in the mid-twenties was exciting! The atmosphere of the Medill School was highly professional; and all around were the big, brassy newspapers of the day. Leland stayed mostly in the YMCAs, downtown or in Evanston. He got a job as assistant editor of the *Epworth Herald*, as Francis had before him; the *Herald* was the official organ of the young peoples' society of the Methodist Church, the Epworth League.

Quite a bit of the instruction at Medill was by seasoned newspapermen from the Chicago area. One who became a friend to Leland in those first months was his teacher in the history of journalism, Elmo Scott Watson. Elmo was editor of *Publishers' Auxiliary*, organ of the Western Newspaper Union, and a feature writer for them. He was eight years older than Leland. He and his wife Julia-Etta made Leland feel welcome at their home.

Elmo had been born on a farm in Lawndale Township, Illinois, and had attended Colorado College. He was one of those men who seem always to make things better around him: he helped organize the Illinois State High School Press Association, the Chicago Scholastic Press Guild, the Industrial Editor's institute, and clinics for news executives. Elmo's life had a considerable influence upon Leland; together they accomplished some significant things, and were friends until Elmo died in 1951.

The Boy Becomes a Man of the World

In addition to his studies, Leland's energy went in a variety of directions in Chicago. He did some work at Jane Addams' Hull House, one of the nation's first social service centers, and helped with a Boy Scout troop. He served on the Official Board of Evanston's First Methodist Church. He worked at helping develop high school journalism. He joined the Acacia Fraternity, where Francis was also a member. The *Northwestern University Alumni News* hired him as managing editor. The Medill School of Journalism promoted him to instructor. All the while, he kept his hand in with Francis and the family in the Black Hills.

Francis had an opportunity to buy the *Hot Springs Times Herald*. Leland helped him with it whenever he could—vacations, a day or two here and there. Their elder sister Joyce had married an attorney, Cliff Wilson, and settled there as well, so Hot Springs became a focus for them all.

This was a period of growth for Leland. He had one foot in the Black Hills that he loved so much and one in America's second city with all of its dynamism. What a time to be alive!

He received his Master of Arts degree from Northwestern University in the spring of 1926, and that summer he seized an opportunity to help conduct a group of Northwestern students on a trip to Europe. They sailed on July third from New York on the S. S. Leviathan, pride of the United States Lines, bound for Southampton via Cherbourg.

There were 75 students and faculty in the tour group. They visited ten European countries in six weeks. Leland and Paul Teetor, an Acacia fraternity brother, decided at the end of the tour to really see France. Knowing their return tickets on the United States Line were good for a year, they looked for jobs at the three American newspapers then published in Paris.

THE MAN FROM THE HILLS

Lawrence Hills of the Paris edition of the *New York Herald* offered Leland a job when one of his key men left the paper. Leland surprised himself by bargaining that he couldn't take the job unless Paul was hired too. What was Teetor's experience? He had worked for a daily in Ottowa, Kansas (although Leland did not feel obliged to specify that the work consisted of an early morning paper route). They were both hired.

The first night on the job, while waiting for the City Editor to check his first copy, his eye happened to catch a rough-penciled list of names on the boss's desk. "Those the people killed in today's train wreck at Fontainbleau?" he asked. "Yes, and a couple of them might be English or American. Know any of them?" Leland took the list back to his desk and studied it. Surely one was the tanned young fellow from near St. Louis who had guided the Northwestern University party through the League of Nations building in Geneva a few weeks before. Yes, the train was from Geneva, the City Editor confirmed. This looked like an angle.

Leland finished his work, which mainly consisted that night of waiting across town at a telegraph office for the results of a boxing match in New York—which never came. Early in the morning, with no sleep, Leland set off by train for Fontainbleau. With very little French but with gestures and persistence, he worked his way into the morgue, identified the body, dug into the details and wrote the story. The victim had been popular in Geneva and prominent at home, and the story hit the wires.

On his first pay-day, Leland's received 100 francs more than what they had agreed upon. Leland was now established at the *Herald*.

It is interesting to notice how easily Leland, the circuit-rider's kid from Iowa and South Dakota, moved into new experiences on a larger stage. Chicago—a transatlantic steamer—Paris! When my own life took adventurous, expansive leaps like these I felt them keenly, talked about the romance of it all, wrote about them to family and friends. Yet nowhere in any of Leland's writings at the time or afterward do you ever get the feeling that these moves were not the most natural thing in the world.

The adventure was not lost on Leland's elder sister Joyce, however. In a letter to Leland in September, she wrote: "I have been waiting ever since 3rd of July, A.D. 1926 to get a letter from my little brother and I am still waiting. You are sure one smart boy. You are going to have a wonderful experience and one that will be an education in itself. Just one thing, Leland, please don't bring any French girls back with you.

"What is there I can send you when you are so far away? I'm afraid cookies wouldn't keep that long, or would they. Esther writes you are sending her a dress. How do you dare to pick out such an article for the female species?

"I am not saying how much work the three youngsters can make. Allen (her son) is always saying something about Uncle Leland—especially how he wants to eat a lot so he will be tall like Uncle Leland. Lois took it into her head she wanted to be like Uncle Leland too, so she cut off all her hair so that she would look like a boy.

"What do you think of your brother taking unto himself a wife? Don't you go and do likewise. I haven't seen the girl good enough for you yet. Here's a world of love for my little brother who is making a big place for himself in this old world. Wish I were half as smart."

While Leland was in Europe Francis, back in South Dakota, had married Myrle Graves, of Mitchell, whom he had met in their college days at Dakota Wesleyan. He was hard at work as one of the prominent young businessmen of the Black Hills. In search of something that would promote the Hills nationwide, he initiated a bold plan with the chamber of commerce and then with the state legislature and the South Dakota delegation in Washington. He kept his brother in Paris appraised of the proposition.

When a piece appeared in the *Paris Herald* raising the question of where the president of the United States, Calvin Coolidge, would spend the summer, analyzing the possibilities and raising the Black Hills as a strong contender, Leland's pals laughed at him. The laughter faded when Coolidge announced that that was where he would vacation. Francis's work had paid off handsomely for the local economy and prestige. Leland's intimate knowledge of the Black Hills enabled the *Herald* to keep its readers informed of all the colorful details of a summer spent there. Francis was given due credit for his enterprise and for his devotion to the public welfare. This was his first major step forward on an outstanding public career.

The months in Paris were full and rich. There was a fair amount of turnover at the *Paris Herald*, and Leland advanced quickly from copy reader to reporter to City Editor. One of his shipmates on the *Leviathan* had been a vivacious young woman from Seattle, Aleda Turbill, and around Paris she and Leland and some of his pals from the *Herald* had a lively social life.

It was a time that was full of the eternal attraction of Paris— the Left Bank, the bistros and cafes, the artists and the beauty of the city. Paul Teetor, Aleda and Leland did a lot of it together. They attended opera, explored the city together and the surrounding countryside, and "we eat much, drink little, and sleep." They helped promote the annual dinner that the Anglo-French Press Association gave for sundry leaders of Paris as well as for their own delight, and that year their featured performer was Josephine Baker.

At the same time Leland kept in touch with Harry Harrington, Director of the Medill School of Journalism. With his record as managing editor of the *Alumni News* in mind, as well as his teaching experience, Leland wrote a proposal for intertwining on-the-job training in writing and editing with the publicity-public relations needs of Northwestern.

"In fact," he wrote, "it has always seemed to me illogical that the two were separate when co-ordination would obviously be to the advantage of each." With a school full of young cub reporters, he said, Medill had much to give the University in exchange for the training the students would receive. He was eager to have a part in developing the idea. He then discussed salary based on his Masters degree, experience, willingness to work, and a host of ideas he had for helping to develop the school further.

The French—and most of the rest of the world—were energized by the race to see who would be the first to fly the Atlantic ocean nonstop. A pair of seasoned French aviators, Charles M. Nungesser and Francois Coli, both World War I flying heroes, had taken off from their side headed for New York. The Paris papers had their triumphal landing all set in type, when their plane disappeared in the north Atlantic and was never heard of again. To pile insult upon injury, the newswires crackled with young, unknown Charles Lindbergh's plans to leave Floyd Bennett Field early one morning and attempt the feat in a tiny plane, alone.

As the fever of anticipation mounted in Paris, a singular fact made it palpable to the French. Lindy's plane had been christened "The Spirit of St. Louis," after the city that had financed his venture. But St. Louis was a much- loved saint in France, and when the shy young man landed at LeBourget, the crowd, the press, and the nation took him to their hearts. The *Herald* assigned Ralph Barnes to cover the story and get an interview.

Overnight the staff at the *Herald* got a wire from the home office. One of their advertisers, the Goodrich Tire Company, wanted confirmation that their tires had lofted and landed the little Ryan aircraft. Leland D. Case was the man available. Getting an interview with Lindbergh was next to impossible; Barnes had had to bluff his way into the American Ambassador's residence and find the Lone Eagle dressed in the ambassador's over-sized pajamas, to get his.

Leland decided on a sneak approach. Lindy was to appear for a ceremony at the Aero Club de France. Leland slipped past a guard and made his way up into the ceremonial salon. There he found the flustered celebrity being asked in French to step out onto the balcony to receive the cheers of the crowd below in the street. Leland, whose French was atrocious but bold, stepped beside him, translated the gist of what was being said to him, and went with him and the dignitaries out onto the balcony. The historic news photo that hit the papers and the newsreels shows Lindy and Ambassador Myron Herrick, with Leland between them interpreting to the hero. And in the process, when asked the advertiser's question, Lindy replied "Goodrich Silvertown Cords."

Back home in Hot Springs, all the Cases and Wilsons went to the movie house to see Uncle Leland in the Fox Movietone News—over and over again. Leland scrounged a few frames of that newsreel from the agency and had the key frame printed

Paris, April 1927—balcony of the Aero Club de France, left to right—Charles Lindbergh, Leland Case, U.S. Ambassador Myron Herrick (from a frame of newsfilm obtained by Leland afterwards in New York—believed to be Fox Movietone News)

up. That photograph has hung on the wall of every office he occupied after that and hangs in his home in Tucson today.

The months in Paris yielded other fruit that was to enrich the rest of Leland's life. He was privileged to meet Louis, le Comte de Lasteyrie, head of the Lafayette family. The count was intelligent, impoverished, lonely, and master of le Chateau LaGrange. The chateau had been Lafayette's home, and was 30 miles southeast of Paris. Together the count and Leland explored the dilapidated chateau, which was almost in ruins. There had been almost no literary antiquities of Lafayette to survive; his grandmother, an English woman, hated the Marquis because he fought against her Good King George III in the American Revolution and she had disposed of all his papers, pictures and books. One newspaper of the day was found

35

on Lafayette's table at his death, and this the count gave to Leland.

Over the years Leland maintained his friendship with the old man. When Louis died in 1955, his nephew, Count Rene de Chambrun, took over LaGrange. Chambrun was wealthy, being of the family that owned Baccarat glass; he restored the chateau and maintained it as a museum. In the donjon tower he found all of the Lafayette memorabilia, miraculously preserved, which the grandmother had apparently locked away all those years before. Leland kept up a friendship with Chambrun as he had with his uncle.

Leland had a couple of letters from Charley Ward, executive secretary of the General Alumni Association of Northwestern University, for whom he worked when writing for the *Alumni News*. Ward was contemplating a trip to Europe; would Case be able to point him to the highlights? Leland replied that he would be glad to help Ward see something of Paris. His comment to Ward about the effect Lindbergh was having on France was, "That tow-headed kid with the platinum pointed nerves has done more to create Franco-American amity than any man since Franklin—and, I might add, pandemonium in this office."

The December 1927 issue of the *Northwestern University Alumni News* carried an account by Charley Ward of an evening with Case "on the town" in Paris.

"We three (Ward, Case and Teetor) started for the old Latin Quarter. Case was the special guide, and a good one. If I could recall for you all that he pointed out and all that he related of history and legend this would be a long story and a good one ... the old church where the massacre of Saint Bartholemew began...derelicts lying under the bridge...the Isle de la Cite...the old Latin Quarter—down a ladder-like stairway in a kind of well, and we arrived in one of those caves that seem to go to make up the underworld of Paris, a low ceiling room of stone, perhaps twenty people present sitting on rude benches beside rough wooden tables on which rested a mug of liquor in front of each person—harlots and men hardly fit to be their companions. And now their entertainment began. It consisted of singing and recitation. At the end of each performance a collection was taken. Folk songs and old folk tales...moderation and restraint... a kind of instinctive dignity."

They didn't get in until 6 A.M., but Charley Ward had seen something of Leland Case's Paris.

To my mind, this is one of the most revealing vignettes of Leland's whole life. What would you expect three young men to see, experience and remember in 1920s Paris? The Folies Bergere? What sticks in Charlie Ward's memory that Leland showed him that night is the innate dignity of down-and-outs in a Paris cavern.

Leland might well have stayed longer in Paris, but Harry Harrington broke his leg on a summer trip in Belgium and urged Leland to return to Medill and take his classes for him for the year.

By September Leland was in the thick of things again at Medill. He not only had Harrington's classes to teach, but he did lectures and seminars for the journalist profession, the Inland Press Association and others. Occasionally he substituted for Elmo Scott Watson, whose work at the Western Newspaper Union kept him busy. Leland found time to tuck in graduate work in anthropology and sociology, as well as continuing to serve on the board of the Evanston Methodist Church, and to keep touch with Hot Springs.

Then there was the great Black Hills oil boom. One Saturday over Edgemont way, near the Wyoming line, somebody spotted oil at an old test hole that had been drilled years before. The *Hot Springs Times Herald* wired the story across the state. Francis organized a couple of little oil companies. Leland and Cliff Wilson put together a mutual investment trust called Western Securities. Francis and Leland put out the *Oil and Mining Journal*, which continued for quite a while. The only thing that didn't pan out was the oil. There just wasn't very much there. But a sense of economic opportunity had been born that persisted.

Leland put a little money into these ventures with Francis. And he worked closely with his brother when he made his first run for public office in 1928. They fought a good, but losing, fight. In that campaign and throughout his political career, Francis made it a contest of issues, not personalities, and built a tremendous reputation as a fair, decent and dedicated man.

Leland's poetry was becoming more sophisticated. This one was dated Hot Springs, Christmas Night, 1928.

THE CATHEDRAL OF ALL MEN
Hush.
>   Of stone and steel
Mortals roof temples for the few,
>   But arched o'er me is a boundless dome
Of whose merest mechanics
>   Wise men guess.
Hush.

***

A yellow rose window is aflame tonight
>   In the Cathedral of All Men.

CHAPTER III
The Man Finds His Professional Career and His Wife

Early in 1928 Leland wrote to The Macmillan Company in New York. Five years earlier they had published a definitive text that was in use at the Medill School of Journalism and in many other schools—*Editing the Day's News* by the late Medill professor George C. Bastian. During that five years, there had been quite a bit of change in the profession of journalism and in the teaching of it. Leland offered to revise the book in order to keep it a leader in the field. Macmillan replied that there was sufficient supply of the text to meet the current demand and they had no plans at the moment to reissue the book.

These were interesting, formative days for Leland Case. He was casting about for the exact direction his career and his life should take. He had his work at Medill. He had work any time he wanted it with Francis in Hot Springs, where the two brothers were co-publishers. He was doing graduate work in sociology at Northwestern and editing its alumni magazine.

That summer he made a proposal to the executives of the Chicago World's Fair Centennial Celebration. This group was preparing their international exposition of 1933—The Century of Progress, and they were looking for models for how their fair should be produced. Leland suggested that the International Press Exhibition, called "Pressa," taking place in Cologne, Germany, would offer some worthwhile possibilities for Chicago. "Pressa" was the first-ever major exposition of the art and history of printing.

Leland was provided with a letter of introduction from the Chicago World's Fair commission requesting that he be given the opportunity of studying the way Pressa had been set up and how themes were carried out. To help pay his way, Leland combined his duties for the Chicago World's Fair with those of a guide for another European tour that he put together himself.

When he returned to Chicago, Leland presented the World's Fair commission with a 119-page report, in which he analyzed the philosophy and psychology of "Pressa" and how its techniques might be applied to the Chicago venture. The report is characteristic of the thorough, idea-based, articulate, imaginative work Leland was to complete throughout his life.

After these projects, Leland did some consulting work in public relations for Chicago firms. He also compiled a 21-page "Inventory of Agencies that Gather and Distribute European News." He considered studying for a doctorate, focusing on the influence of propaganda and public relations upon public opinion and to what degree this might be an insidious manipulation of the public mind.

One evening he was invited to a dinner party at the home of a woman who was a member of the faculty at Northwestern University. He was seated opposite a small, vivacious young lady with a melodious voice. Her name was Josephine Altman, and she was teaching music appreciation at the New Trier High School in Evanston.

Discovering that she lived nearby, Leland offered to walk her home after the party. That was the beginning of a 57 year relationship that ended only with Leland's death. A few days after the dinner party Leland learned that Josephine and her roommate had been bothered by someone in the neighborhood. Leland moved to an apartment near them to be their guard, she would always say later.

The Man Finds His Professional Career and His Wife

In the spring of 1929 he was in Hot Springs helping Francis transform the weekly *Hot Springs Star* into a tabloid daily and wrestling with how to get more mileage out of the oil-strike incident. Josephine Altman was on his mind considerably, and he sent her a stream of enticing literature on his favorite corner of the world. He enlisted the family to work up an appropriate invitation for her to join them for a visit. The *Star* printed the invitation for him—with Mrs. Joyce Wilson as Chairman of the Committee on Housing, Francis the Committee on Fraternal Relations, and Leland as Chairman of the Entertainment Committee.

When Miss Altman stepped off the train at Buffalo Gap, Leland was there with the old Ford, "Wounded Knee", and his dog Pinto as his reception committee. They had bought her a buckskin gown in Rapid City, and they posed her for a photo in which she wore the dress with her long black braids, at Kidney Springs (which the more high-brow liked to refer to as "Hygeia Springs"). She giggled with glee when the photo was used not only in the *Star*, but also in Chamber of Commerce literature.

Josephine was interested in the music of various ethnic and national groups and had studied voice in Milan, Fontainbleau, Stockholm, and the National Museum of Mexico. Her father, Dr. Frank DeGraff Altman, taught at Midland College Lutheran Seminary in Atchison, Kansas, where she had been born. The seminary and the Altmans were later relocated to Fremont, Nebraska. Josephine had received a degree from the University of Nebraska, where she had earned a Phi Beta Kappa key.

The climax of her two-week visit to Hot Springs was her participation in a Sioux dance on the porch of the Evans Hotel. An ancient chief named Henry White Man Bear was charmed by her presence, and in his enthusiasm adopted her as his daugh-

41

Hot Springs, SD 1929 Josephine Altman being adopted by Henry White Man Bear, Ogalala Sioux, giving her the name Zitkaziwin, Yellow Singing Bird

ter. He gave her the name "Zitkaziwin," or "Yellow Singing Bird", in recognition not only of her voice but also of her interest in Indian songs. She would listen intently to their singing and write down phonetically what she heard. In following years she was to learn a great deal about Indian music and song and added much music from various tribes to her repertoire.

For some time Leland had been interested in the story of Preacher Smith. His research had led him to collect files about Henry Weston Smith. Smith had been born in 1827 in Ellington, Connecticut. He trained as a Methodist preacher, saw service in the Civil War, and in 1876 had followed the gold seekers to the Black Hills. In the brawling mining camp which was Deadwood in its gold-rush heyday, Smith preached the gospel on the streets because he had no church. In August, 1876, he left his cabin in Deadwood, crossed the pass to Crook City for a Sunday service, and never returned. A few hours later his body was found on the road above town, strangely lying at peace with his hands folded on his chest.

The press of the day reported that Smith had been ambushed by Indians. Many others, at the time of the murder and thereafter, felt that it was even more likely that he had been killed by elements in the town who favored the wide-open lawless atmosphere then prevailing. A Sioux named Turning Bear, one report went, had confessed to the sheriff at Deadwood that he had killed the preacher; there was a white man, according to another story, who claimed to have done it.

In the summer of 1929, Leland wrote a speech about Smith for Francis to give in Deadwood. Leland asked for and took no credit for the speech, but did it to help his brother. Over the years Leland ghosted several things for Francis, including a book on managing public relations for churches. Both Francis and Leland not only took their church work seriously, but they also took being brothers seriously.

When he was in Hot Springs, Leland usually stayed with Francis and Myrle, where his dog Pinto also had his home. Sister Joyce and her husband Cliff Wilson now had three children—Allen, Lois and Dorothy.

For Christmas, 1929, the children had a real live visit from Santa Claus. Leland was staying with them for the holidays. During the night the family heard a commotion up on the roof. They all ran outside, and there was Santa Claus! He had fallen out of his airplane onto their house! Everyone, including the neighbors, came out in their pajamas to see. Pinto was there, barking and barking at Santa, and Joyce told the children that it was because Pinto didn't like Santa's red suit. Of course it was really because Pinto recognized Leland underneath that costume. Santa came down a ladder with his bag of toys and had something for each of them.

In 1930 Leland wrote again to The Macmillan Company. *Editing the Day's News* really needs to be revised, he said, or it will decline in value and in its place in the textbook field. "I began making notes on revision," he told them, "when I succeeded Professor Bastian in teaching the course, which he had instituted at Medill." This time the Macmillan people were interested. T. C. Morehouse of Macmillan's college department wrote to Leland. Arrangements were made with the author's widow for permission to revise the text and to divide the 10 percent royalty equally with Leland. The work got under way.

In the middle of all this work came an offer that established Leland's career for the next 35 years. He was invited to join the staff of *The Rotarian*, the magazine of Rotary International, even though he was not a Rotarian.

Paul Harris, a quiet, industrious lawyer from Wisconsin and Vermont, had moved into the busy hard-headed world of Chicago commerce around the turn of the century. He felt the need for comradeship and the reinforcement of his personal ideals. In 1905 he invited three men to meet with him one evening for fellowship and to support each other in their careers. At the second meeting each thought of others who might be included, and the idea mushroomed. The group adopted the name Rotary from their original practice of rotating the meeting place among the members' office locations. By 1910 the idea had spread to 14 other American cities and was on its way to becoming the service-club concept that is so well established today.

Paul Harris, the founder and conceptualizer of the Rotarian idea, had his counterpart in Chesley R. Perry, the organizer and builder of it. Perry had joined the Chicago club in 1908, and had quickly grasped what this young movement could mean. He was a very well-organized person, who injected that quality into everything that involved Rotary, becoming its General Secretary.

Ches Perry realized the need for a publication, not just for the plentiful club news, but also for articles by influential leaders as well. The magazine which became *The Rotarian* appeared in January 1911, with Perry as its publisher and editor. It was supported by membership dues. As the organization grew, the magazine became too much for the General Secretary to handle, and in 1927 the board of directors of Rotary decided to create a separate staff for *The Rotarian*.

It took more than five years for this concept to develop to the satisfaction of the board. Vivian John Carter, a professional journalist from Rotary in Great Britain, was hired as editor, but the board was dissatisfied with his work. Emerson Gause, who had worked with Ches Perry on the magazine since 1916, replaced Carter. The board respected Gause's professional competence, but desired an editor with a more dynamic style of leadership, if such a person could be found.

The board advertised in *Editor & Publisher* for an experienced man who could head "an idealistic magazine, would understand how to obtain readers' interest and be resourceful and constructive. Salary up to $10,000." The editor would have full control, subject to the general supervision of a Magazine Committee, which would report to the board of directors. At the same time, as Ches Perry often said, there was an on-going debate within the board over the character of the magazine—and that very same debate goes on in 1994: Is this to be a Rotarian "house organ," or a general businessmen's magazine, or something in between?

The new magazine committee appointed Douglas C. McMurtrie, a prominent typographer and associate professor at The Medill School of Journalism, to be executive counselor for *The Rotarian*. They determined that the scope of the magazine should be gradually "broadened and more international." In July of 1930, Clinton P. Anderson, a South Dakotan, was appointed chairman of the magazine committee of the board of directors.

Anderson and Leland Case's elder sister Joyce had been classmates at Dakota Wesleyan University. They both attended college on a shoestring, and had shared textbooks; they would leave books under a rock on campus for each other to pick up. Clint Anderson was well-acquainted with the Cases of DWU—Joyce, Francis, and Leland. He was now in business in Albuquerque, New Mexico, where he had located to recover from tuberculosis.

I have not uncovered any clue as to how Leland was introduced to *The Rotarian*. It is quite possible that he responded to the ad in *Editor & Publisher*. Anderson may have had a hand in it, or McMurtrie might have accomplished it through his work at the Medill School. However it came about, in July of 1930, Leland D. Case was hired by *The Rotarian* and by October he was listed as assistant editor.

What the organization hired was one of the brightest products of the Medill School of Journalism, with academic experience well-balanced by eight or nine years in the rough-

and-tumble world of working to daily deadlines and to the demands of competition in the marketplace. Today he would be called a workaholic. He was at home in the world and with people of every stripe. As Rotary was entering its second quarter-century, Leland became the right man for its chief organ of communication and information, in which he was keen to put all of his ideas, convictions, and experience to work.

The records available at the headquarters of Rotary International on this period of *The Rotarian* are sketchy. I spent a week there, digging for the story. As I piece it together, I can imagine Leland moving into this very promising situation and feeling his way forward. He respected Douglas McMurtrie, and their friendship lasted until the older man died in 1944. Leland was assistant to Emerson Gause, and the test of Leland's tact and ingenuity seemed to have been finding a way to introduce fresh ideas without causing ill feeling. It apparently worked, as the next few months showed.

Leland's first meeting with Chesley Perry, the general secretary, was on a decidedly informal note. Eager to get on with his new job, Leland arrived at the Rotary International offices on Wacker Drive on a hot, humid Saturday, sat down at his desk, and peeled off his shirt. "I became aware of a baldheaded male beside my desk—grinning," Leland said later. "I see you've stripped for action," he quipped. "Good! We should get acquainted because we'll probably be working together quite awhile. I'm Ches Perry."

Working on a Saturday was not surprising for either man. Perry was as hard-working as they come, and Leland had learned early that, especially in a busy office, Saturday was a good day to get things done. He worked Saturdays more often than not throughout his entire career, and sometimes Sundays as well.

THE MAN FROM THE HILLS

The influence of Leland Davidson Case was felt in the magazine at once. The October issue carried a story by "Lee Davidson" on the need to consider humanely the beggars who were being driven to the streets by The Depression.

The Depression was the great overriding fact of the 1930s, in America and in all of the industrial countries of the world. It has been the worst and longest economic downturn the United States has ever experienced. In most respects it lasted 10 years. Those of us who lived through The Depression sometimes are amazed at what people today think are bad economic conditions.

Leland's story in the October, 1930, issue of *The Rotarian* was the first of dozens of articles he wrote for the magazine, most of them under his own by-line. In the 1930s those stories most often were concerned with how communities were dealing with the economic crisis, usually by finding their own solutions; how families were coping with tight budgets; what innovative new practices businesses were developing in order to survive; all aimed at helping Rotary people everywhere lead in morale and economic recovery.

Leland did a story for the December, 1930, issue about a trip he took to a Kalamazoo paper mill called "Where Ideas Turn Wheels." The story told of the efficient use of manpower in the mill, strongly emphasizing how employee suggestions were keeping the mill running at capacity despite the hard times. Employee ideas had produced a line of wrapping paper to protect food sold in retail stores from germs (a new idea for the time!); excelsior-stuffed paper stadium seats for use during football games on cold days; paper tablecloths; paper wipes; and the idea of selling paper in rolls to housewives.

48

The Man Finds His Professional Career and His Wife

Most of these stories derived from field trips Leland had taken to get the facts and the feel of economic situations first hand, and they all represented the wonderful way he had of meeting new people. By the time he had been on the staff for a year he had made trips to Michigan, Indiana, Tennessee, Washington D.C., Pennsylvania, and New York. On most of these trips he had addressed local Rotary Clubs about the magazine's attempts to help them cope with The Depression.

Leland's energy and imagination could be felt everywhere in the offices of *The Rotarian*. Take for instance how they promoted the magazine through other print media. Press releases were circulated to some 2000 North American newspapers, releases that carried extracts of articles in current editions of the magazine. In the first three months of this practice over 500 *Rotarian* articles were carried in 450 different newspapers. Or take his strong belief in graphics. He influenced the magazine committee to use more illustrations—photos, drawings, and original art work.

During all this, Leland kept his promise to Macmillan's editors. Feeling his way for what was really wanted, he made some suggestions about inexpensive "plate patches" for his changes in the text. T. C. Morehouse replied that they desired a complete resetting of the type for the text, since they wanted a thorough revision of the book.

Leland necessarily did most of his revision of *Editing the Day's News* in the evenings. He added 12 pages of photographs to emphasize the growing importance of photography to modern-day journalism. The massive amounts of detail in Leland's work were impressive. He specified typefaces, paging, and indentations for effect. There were almost daily letters between

49

New York and Chicago carrying his suggestions or requests and the publisher's almost total acceptance of his ideas.

On July 28, 1931, Leland Case and Josephine Altman were married. The party journeyed to Knoxville, Tennessee, to the home of Josephine's sister, Mrs. Homer P. Shepherd. The bride wore her sister's wedding gown of ivory charmeuse, and carried a bouquet of yellow roses. Her widowed mother gave her away; her sister's two daughters were her attendants; Homer Shepherd was Leland's best man. It was a quiet wedding, with only family and intimate friends as witnesses.

Leland and Josephine drove through New England on their honeymoon. They discovered in each other a love of such things as old stained glass. They stopped in Philadelphia to visit the D'Ascenzo studio, where stained glass masterpieces were being made using the methods of the Middle Ages. One memento of that visit was a piece the D'Ascenzo studio made for them of "The Nativity," which still hangs in the living room window of their home in Tucson.

Back in Chicago, they stayed for a time in Evanston at the Homestead, a gracious hotel designed, built, and owned by architect Philip A. Danielson, with whom Leland was to have a friendship over many years.

Leland filed every scrap of paper on his revision of *Editing the Day's News*—correspondence, the galley proofs, the sources of his facts. He would go to any lengths to get the book right and as up to date as possible. He sent paragraphs or sections of his draft to men whom he considered to be authorities on particular subjects, such as working newspapermen, typesetters, linotype experts or manufacturers, magazine editors, and professors. He asked their opinions, and checked facts and details.

The Man Finds His Professional Career and His Wife

He included other's writing in the text, reprinting exemplary passages from other authors, and was willing to pay fees for what he used. The monetary returns he expected or received in later years in no way compensated for the effort he exerted to produce the best textbook on the subject.

The editors at Macmillan had to keep prodding him, very courteously, because all of this took time. "I have endeavored to keep changes to a minimum consistent with our purpose of making the revision one which will command professional respect and serve as the standard text of its time," he wrote to them, and in the same letter pointed the typesetter's mistake of replacing Cheltenham typeface with a form of Caslon. The changes and enhancements over the first edition were so great that Mrs. Bastian's attorney suggested its chief opinions were not those of George Bastian, so therefore the name of Leland Case should be played up to indicate his status as an author rather than as an editor.

After the deadline passed, Leland asked the publishers for permission to revise a paragraph in which he had included a trade rumor that the *Chicago Tribune* was installing 12-color presses, a huge advance in the field. Leland found a reliable inside source at the *Tribune* and learned that it was actually using five-color equipment. That change was readily accepted by Macmillan.

The textbook was published in late April of 1932, just in time to compete for the fall semester's market. For the last couple of months, there had been daily letters dealing with intricate details. A person less diligent and driving probably could not have accomplished the task, but Leland thrived on this kind of activity.

Then the publisher's staff and Leland went to work on getting the book reviewed and adopted in colleges and universities. Leland compiled lists of people to receive review copies, wrote to most of them himself, and waited eagerly for reviews to be printed and the orders to come in. By the fall of 1932, 55 schools had ordered the book. A year later the count was 92.

The staff at Macmillan wrote to Leland expressing how they appreciated working with him. Leland wrote his thanks to all who had helped him, and he sent a note to Mrs. Bastian saying what a privilege it had been to work on her husband's book.

By the end of 1931 Douglas McMurtrie could report to the magazine committee at Rotary that morale at the magazine staff was high and cooperation smooth. At the same time, he said, the staff was overworked, and they were publishing far more articles by outside authors than they would like because they didn't have the time to write their own that would be tailored specifically for Rotary. The committee was concerned to give the staff leeway "for inspirational thought." They had effected a good many economies, including a cut in their own salaries as well as the entire Rotary International staff, which kept expenses under budget. Income for the year came from members dues, which included the magazine's subscription price, and from the sale of advertising, and totaled about $254,000, with expenses of around $243,000.

The official Rotary directory for 1932 listed an editorial board for *The Rotarian* consisting of McMurtrie, Emerson Gause, and Leland Case. Leland arranged for his friend Paul Teetor, from *Paris Herald* days and who had in the meantime been managing editor for the *Northwestern University Alumni News*, to join *The Rotarian* as assistant editor.

The Man Finds His Professional Career and His Wife

The role of *The Rotarian* was to inspire the members of the movement, and to represent the movement to the world. In notes prepared for a staff meeting, Leland established a leadership position for himself in this effort. *"The Rotarian,"* he said, "is OUR magazine—yours. Rotary is no longer an infant organization. It is a strong organization. It has a proud record, a record to be vindicated by future service. We believe the magazine should reflect this. It should more than deal with those interests of an infant club—but should discuss in a mature way the interests that business and professional men have, not within the favored circle of the club, but in the great outside world of events and affairs. That is why I am here."

The editorial staff worked hard to stay in tune with the thoughts of the men in the local clubs. Every three months each of the editorial staff spent time sampling the opinions of the readership. The staff member would visit a club and make a talk about the magazine, and then, using the club roster, would endeavor to speak with every member in person. A couple of recent issues of the magazine would be reviewed with the member page by page by asking such things as did you read that story, what did you think of it? Notes from these sessions helped the staff determine that about 60 percent of the members in their samples should be classified as "readers." This figure was high in the magazine industry. They found that the general preference was for subjects concerning business and economics, followed by travel, and then Rotary activities.

Clint Anderson served as president of Rotary International for 1932-33. Anderson showed Leland two letters he had received, each from a Rotarian, in which opposite viewpoints had been taken on the question of federal support for agriculture. Leland's response was, "Why not use our pages for controversial issues—take no side ourselves, but let important men state their convictions." He suggested they then follow this with readers' comments in succeeding editions. Thus was created one of the most durable and popular features of *The Rotarian*—the debate-of-the-month. There are still several debates-of-the month in the magazine each year.

Leland worked closely with Anderson, who devoted a great deal of time to the magazine. Anderson believed that the editor should have a free hand, not only in what appeared in the pages of the magazine but in the matter of staffing and salaries. He asked how a board of directors could know the relative merits of people on the staff and their relation to the field of journalism. Board members come and go; an editor is selected because he knows his stuff, and he should be expected to exercise his good professional judgment within the agreed upon budget.

By the end of Anderson's term as Rotary International president, the magazine's board of editors was listed as Leland Case, Emerson Gause, and Paul Teetor, in that order.

The staff worked hard to promote *The Rotarian*. They were successful in having it accepted for inclusion in the reading racks of trains, steamships, and airlines. They experimented with Christmas gift subscriptions. A demand and interest in the magazine was steadily growing outside of the membership of Rotary. This is still true, when *The Rotarian* has over 25,000 subscriptions from non-Rotarians.

During Anderson's presidency, Rotary started publication of a Spanish-language version of their magazine—*Revista Rotaria*. Manuel Hinojosa Flores, of Mexico, was hired to work under Leland in publishing the magazine, a job he held for many years.

The Man Finds His Professional Career and His Wife

Walter Dunlap was another chairman of the magazine committee who took his role seriously. Dunlap was an advertising executive from Milwaukee. As a practical man, he apparently recognized that Leland was the key to the effective operation of the staff and that the concept of an "editorial board" controlling the magazine was effective only until Leland was established both within the magazine staff and with the Rotary board of directors.

Typical of Leland's work in those days was the report he drafted for Dunlap to present to the board in January of 1934. Dunlap signed the report, but the tone and verbiage are distinctly Leland Case's.

"Normal practice," the report said, "is that readers buy the magazine that fits them. With *TR* [insider language for *The Rotarian*], the magazine is designed to fit the readers. The great bulk of those who join Rotary have the motive of being served by the organization, not to serve. *TR* needs to educate them." You on the Board of Directors of Rotary, the report to them said, are, frankly, not the audience we are writing for. We are writing to stimulate enthusiasm for and understanding of Rotary among the men in the ranks who need that stimulation.

The report cited surveys the staff were taking under Leland's direction. From the surveys, they had developed a very definite emphasis on human-interest stories, stories about people—the more prominent the better. Controversy, in the debate-of-the month format, was very popular. Add inspiration—just a dash, was their policy, as well as humor, adventure, entertainment—just enough to keep a balance.

The report went on to compare circulations of the major intellectual and business journals for 1934—*Atlantic*, 103,907; *Scribners*, 45,095; *Harpers*, 92,014; *Forbes*, 53,192; *Fortune*,

73,136; *The Rotarian*, 115,992.

And the report cited another of Leland's innovations, a contract with *Readers Digest*, exclusive for this type of magazine, for the *Digest* to carry a minimum of four *TR* articles per year, for a yearly fee to *TR* of $400 plus $100 for each additional article carried. At that time the *Digest* had 300,000 readers.

During Chairman Dunlap's tenure, he was especially concerned about the depth of the magazine's editorial manpower. If Leland should become ill, or if he were lured away by a better offer, Dunlap reasoned, it would be a very great loss, unless they had an adequate understudy. Leland had told Dunlap, after the fact, that he had turned down a fine position with Armour Company. Dunlap's response was to seek a salary increase for Leland.

A few months later (August, 1934), having spent considerable time with Leland, Dunlap reported to Rotary President Bob Hill, "We need to assume that LDC will continue this, literally a life work, at least for the next eight or ten years. Leland says he has turned down other offers and plans to stay. He puts in much overtime and is carrying the major part of the editorial load." Although Dunlap considered that he himself was responsible for quite a bit of the improvement in management at *TR*, "the major part of credit for the editorial advancement of the publication belongs to Mr. Case."

By January of 1935 Dunlap had formalized his conviction that Leland was the man on whom to build the future of the magazine, and Leland was named Editor of *The Rotarian*.

Part of the answer to Walter Dunlap's concerns, and to the need to relieve some of Leland Case's load, was Leland's own efforts to build up a bright, effective staff for *The Rotarian*. He met and interviewed people frequently and mulled over the make-up of his team.

One of the men sent to Leland for an interview was Karl Krueger. When the magazine committee, in response to Dunlap's urging, authorized the hiring of an assistant for Leland, Krueger was the man he eventually picked. Krueger had been born and raised in Sioux Falls, South Dakota, which did no harm with Leland Case. He had been teaching English and journalism at Sioux Falls College.

It was a spring day when Leland phoned from Chicago to ask if Krueger could drop what he was doing and come at once, with a salary of $175 a month after a probationary period. Krueger was earning $85 a month at the college. "Could I come!," was the reply, "I'll get somebody to finish out the spring semester and be there on Saturday!"

Krueger arrived on that Saturday, when officially the offices of Rotary International were closed. But as in his own first Saturday on the job, Leland was there at his desk and welcomed the new man. They talked a bit about the job and the organization, and then Leland handed him a big batch of material to proof with the statement that Karl might as well get started. Hours later Karl retired to his room in Evanston, dead tired but thrilled with his new job.

Leland knew one secret of getting the maximum out of the crew of young professionals he was putting together. It was to keep them constantly aware of the magazine's importance to the whole of Rotary and to let them know they were vital to the success of the organization. There was a certain Spartan atmosphere about the offices of Rotary International; Chesley Perry, for instance, had everyone of his hundred or more staff including himself, clock in and out on the time clock each day.

Only the very top executives had their names on their office doors. But Leland had the names of his three key men, Paul Teetor, Karl K. Krueger, and Ainsley H. Roseen, printed on the doors of their offices in letters of gold. They were proud of that distinction, and they worked to live up to it.

After a month on the job, and feeling a bit settled in at *The Rotarian*, Karl Krueger asked Leland for a week-end off in order to get married. At *The Rotarian* you had to plan weekends in advance, because the editorial staff was expected to show up on Saturdays and often on Sundays if previous arrangements had not been made with the boss. Leland was delighted to hear about the impending wedding. Paul Teetor and he took Karl out for the traditional bachelor dinner at a little Howard Street bar where that week there was entertainment supplied by The Beef Trust Girls, a "chorus line" of huge gals weighing maybe 300 pounds each.

Karl's bride Dorothy, also a South Dakotan, was a feisty soul. At a typical working dinner, where several of the wives joined the staff just to have a little time with their husbands, Dorothy asked why the staff was working so hard. Leland responded "Because, Dorothy, it's our duty." "Damn duty!" the new bride exploded. She and Karl always thought that Leland warmed to Dorothy more after that.

Many people like Karl Krueger responded to Leland Case and to the chance to work with him. He instilled in them a respect for the profession and a determination to be the best they could be. Leland was a driver, but most of the staff endured his unspoken expectancy of overtime hours, in which he led the way. Others found this not to their liking; most of them did not stay very long.

The Man Finds His Professional Career and His Wife

The staff knew they were working with an extraordinary man. He had the journalistic savvy that proved to be right far more often than not. Unrufflable, soft-spoken, he was never known to yell at anyone. Always contemporary, he brought back from Europe in the mid-thirties a small camera called a Leica which was revolutionizing news photography. This launched some of his people into careers in magazine photography.

Leland also had connections. He could move confidently into situations of which the rest of the staff were in awe. People at the Rotary headquarters have told me recently, "He could get to people we would never be able to reach." But what were his connections? Certainly not his brother, since these connections existed long before his brother was elected to Congress. Usually, he made the connections himself. Was it gall, brass, or did his ability to make connections simply arise from his conviction about the value of the magazine and the importance of the ablest men in the field speaking to Rotary's membership?

In November of 1934, the offices of Rotary International, and *The Rotarian*, were moved to the Pure Oil Building at 35 Wacker Drive. The masthead read, "Editor, Leland D. Case. Assistant Editor, Paul Teetor. Business and Advertising Manager, Harvey C. Kendall."

May Aaberg's first job out of high school had been working for Francis Case on the *Star* in Hot Springs, her home town. When he had unsuccessfully run a second time for Congress in 1935, she worked for his campaign. Since the campaign had very little money, May had received only enough expense money for food and lodging. Francis felt he was in her debt, and that she was a bright girl who needed broader horizons. He persuaded Leland to give her a try as his secretary.

May had an aunt and uncle in Chicago, and so, at age 20, she took the train to the big city. It was appalling to her—the bustle of Chicago, the size of the Rotary International offices and staff, the pace of the work. She went home to her aunt, wept that she couldn't handle it, and planned to catch the next train home. Her aunt wouldn't hear of it; there was no such thing as "can't." She must tough it out.

On Christmas Eve, Leland called her in to his office—after five o'clock, still at work, to take dictation of a short note. The note was to Francis, which said, "Here at the magazine we don't give Christmas presents to the staff, but dictating this letter to May Aaberg may be a present to her of sorts, because she has proved satisfactory and I would be very happy to have her continue working as my secretary." Working late on Christmas Eve or not, May considered it a real present.

May worked for Leland for eight years, until she joined the Women's Army Corps in the middle of World War II. She was an effective secretary. She, like so many South Dakotans, had studied one year at Dakota Wesleyan, which was the extent of her college education. However, she knew she was gaining an education of great value from Leland and *The Rotarian*, and she saw that as compensation for the long hours.

Leland and Josephine sometimes gave parties for the staff. They might decide on a theme and invite everyone to come in costume. Josephine would sing, or Leland would produce games or skits. Everyone would be drawn into the fun, but no one went home tipsy—because there was no tipple. They were happy parties, nonetheless.

Although Josephine sometimes would allow her own opinion of this to show. "Won't you have some tomato juice. I wish it could be stronger," she'd confide on occasion, "but Leland won't permit it." Leland never made an issue of alcohol as far as I know. In all the years I knew him, whether discussing arrangements for a banquet or reception or during a meal, the subject just never came up.

The Depression influenced the lives of Rotarians as it did everyone else in the country. In individual Rotary clubs, more and more members attended programs to satisfy attendance requirements, but they sat along the walls with comments such as, "I ate early" or "I'm on a diet." Some even brought sack lunches to club meetings. There just was not enough money in peoples' pockets for the lunch that had been the formerly customary thing. Rotary International and *The Rotarian*, sensitive to this catastrophic change in American life and in the fortunes of the business world, worked to keep not only the spirit of Rotary alive, but also the American spirit of personal initiative.

For several years Rotarians had been smarting under attacks from some of the leading intellectuals of the day. George Bernard Shaw, when asked where he thought the Rotary movement was headed, replied, "I know where Rotary is going. It's going to lunch." H. L. Mencken had said some very abrasive things. Sinclair Lewis had written the books *Main Street* and *Babbitt* in which Rotary had taken a severe beating. Once Leland felt that he had the magazine on the track he wanted for it, he decided it was time to deal with these problems.

In the summer of 1935 Leland proposed to Bob Hill, the current magazine committee chairman, to invite these critics to write for *The Rotarian* on topics dear to their hearts. Chairman Hill agreed with the idea, and Leland went to work.

Leland knew that celebrity writers are proud of their work, that their fans are important to them, and that they are loyal to periodicals that publish them. Leland also was fairly certain that these critics really knew very little about Rotary and even

61

less about *The Rotarian*. He decided to send copies of the magazine to them, targeting Clarence Darrow, George Bernard Shaw, Henry L. Mencken, and Sinclair Lewis.

Darrow lived in Chicago, so Leland picked him first. Even though he made an appointment by phone, Leland had to deal with a protective wife to get into the Darrow apartment. Since Attorney Darrow had made a national reputation by defending two murderers and was staunchly opposed to capital punishment, Leland invited him to write the "against" position in a debate-of-the-month on the subject for *The Rotarian*. Darrow agreed, and when his article was ready, Leland personally picked it up so he could talk to Darrow further.

Mencken seemed surprised at an invitation to contribute an article to *The Rotarian*. Leland had corresponded with him on the origin of the expression "OK," and perhaps that had paved the way. In any case, Mencken responded by writing the "yes" side of a debate concerning the abolishment of frills in public education. His opponent was the prestigious philosopher of education, John Dewey, so this panel truly represented the heavy-weights.

The problem with Sinclair Lewis was another matter. Leland and Josephine, in the course of a trip east, drove to Lewis's summer retreat in Vermont. Because of daylight saving time, they arrived at the door thinking it was 9:00 A.M. when it was actually only 8 o'clock. Leland left his wife in the car with the statement, "Only be half an hour."

Lewis's maid politely let him in. After a long wait the author appeared in pajamas, bathrobe and slippers, barking "Who the hell are you? Why are you here? What do you want?" Case barked back that he edited *The Rotarian* and had come all the way from Chicago to find out just what it was that Lewis disliked so much about Rotarians. Lewis gathered his wife, the equally well-known author Dorothy Thompson, to the breakfast table, pulled up a chair for Leland, and said they'd eat first, talk later.

After breakfast Leland reminded Lewis why he had come. "Name just one thing you don't like about Rotary," he challenged. "I don't like their singing," snapped Lewis. "Shake," said Case. "I can never reach 'the home of the brave.' What else?" "Calling strangers by first names," Lewis griped. "I once visited a Rotary near here and right away they were calling me Sinclair—something I hadn't heard since last I saw my mother." Case realized this was an opening. He told Rotary's classic tale of lonely men from small towns speeding up the process of making acquaintances in big bustling Chicago by using first names or nicknames just as they did back home. Leland talked about how the way this first-name business was received in England, Australia, New Zealand, Canada, and China. The world scope of Rotary was news to Lewis.

Four hours later, Leland rejoined his wife in the car, and they headed west toward Chicago. Waiting for Leland at the office on Wacker Drive was a note in Sinclair Lewis's own hand, which because of its landmark significance for Rotarians was reproduced many times in the magazine and other places. It ended, "It was pleasant to see you here. You made me approve of Rotary. Sincerely yours, Sinclair Lewis."

Lewis wrote an article for *The Rotarian* "Don't Paint the Lily" about one of his pet peeves, salespeople's habits of grossly overdoing service and tiring their customers with effusiveness.

Because of limited travel funds, Leland chose to negotiate with George Bernard Shaw's literary agent in New York. Since Hitler and Chamberlain had just met in Munich, *The Rotarian* invited GBS to write on the futility of war. His article "Never Another World War" appeared in the magazine in February, 1939. A news note that may have helped Shaw decide to write the article could well have been a dispatch late in 1937 from Berlin stating that members of the Nazi party must give up membership in Rotary clubs before the end of the year.

As far as Leland was able to discover, neither Darrow, Shaw, Mencken, or Lewis ever made public utterances unfavorable to Rotary again.

In the course of working up the arrangement with Sinclair Lewis for his article, Leland found that the *Readers Digest* was interested in printing something by Lewis. The *Digest* was willing to pay the author's fee in return for rights to reprint the story after it was carried in *The Rotarian*. Leland's correspondent at the *Digest* was Charles Ferguson. They wrote back and forth, and before long they were calling each other "Leland" and "Fergie." From this occasion in 1937, Charles Ferguson and Leland Case remained close friends. Leland's relationship with *Readers Digest* extended to many others on the staff, including *Digest* founder DeWitt Wallace and his wife, Lila Acheson Wallace. Until Wallace died, the two men wrote letters on a friendly, first-name basis.

Chesley Perry wrote a letter to Magazine Committee Chairman Hill early in 1936 in which he stated, "Let's make it more of a Rotary magazine. We can't satisfy the advertisers who want more circulation, so we might as well really serve our own people. Leland Case is a brilliant man and an able editor, and we would have to look a good distance to find anyone to replace him. However, he has one handicap which we ought to try to help him overcome. He is primarily an editor and sec-

The Man Finds His Professional Career and His Wife

In 1935 Leland and Joan Case visited with the distinguished potter Maria Martinez (left) at her home in San Ildefonso Pueblo, NM

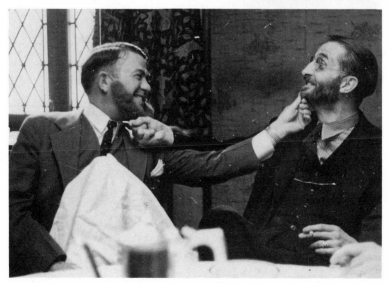

Rotary International president Robert Hill and Leland fooling around about 1934

ondarily a Rotarian. What the magazine needs is someone who is primarily a Rotarian and secondarily an editor." Walter Dunlap, who received a copy of this letter, disagreed emphatically and put it in writing.

Perry did Leland the courtesy of showing him this correspondence, including his own retraction of the idea. Leland thanked the general secretary and assured him that he was following the policy guidelines set by the committee to the best of his abilities and for the good of Rotary.

Although Leland received mainly encouragement from the top eschelons of Rotary, there were definitely people in the leadership who did not agree with Leland's handling of the magazine. Had he not been so clearly motivated toward the best interest of this growing organization and so artful in his presentations to the magazine committee and to the board of directors, it is doubtful that Leland could have developed so outstanding a magazine.

The list of personalities whom Leland included as contributors to *The Rotarian* is legendary. Carlos Romulo, one of the most prominent citizens of the Philippines, was a Rotarian, who wrote for Leland a number of times and became a lifelong friend. Albert Einstein received Leland in his home. Einstein was wary of reporters and interviews, but did reply in German to Leland's written questions.

Others included H. G. Wells, British historian; Charles F. Kettering, one of the founders of General Motors; P. K. Wrigley, world-famous for his chewing gum; Frank Lloyd Wright, America's most widely known architect; Winston Churchill, perhaps Britain's most controversial politician at the time and soon to be her wartime prime minister; Eleanor Roosevelt, social activist wife of the U. S. president; Babe Ruth, baseball's homerun king; Andrei Gromyko, foreign minister of the Soviet Union; and Mahatma Gandhi, who was agitating with his relentless non-violent movement for independence for India from Great Britain.

Now that Rotary International had an editor who could articulate the purpose of *The Rotarian* so well, Leland was scheduled for a great number of appearances at Rotary clubs around the country. He was a featured personality at district and regional meetings, and he attended most of the international conventions. By the middle of 1934 his edition of *Editing the Day's News* was a standard text in 171 schools across the land. In spite of all this he kept up his work for the Medill School, chairing press seminars and round-table discussions. All his activities helped enhance the stature of the magazine.

The Macmillan staff asked Leland to revise *Graded Exercizes in News Writing*, the workbook that they had published to accompany *Editing the Day's News*. He accepted the task that was to be completed before the end of the year. His approach, tempered by the combination of hands-on newspaper and magazine work and his teaching experience, was to break away from anything he had ever seen and "to adapt it functionally," he stated, "to professional practice and pedagogic presentation, to command the respect of 'hardboiled' newspaper men as, I believe, *Editing the Day's News* does; and at the same time to be pedagogically correct".

Leland had seen that workbooks about teaching journalism failed to carry into practice the professional principles that they articulated. Most taught, for instance, the inviolable rule of using a standard size of editorial copy paper, and of writing on only one side of it. However, the usual workbook provided a different size of paper with text printed on both sides. He persuaded Macmillan to print the workbook on only one side of the normal size of copy paper.

A few months later Macmillan asked Leland to revise George Bastian's *Around the Copydesk,* another standard work in their arsenal of textbooks. Feeling the weight of his daily work on *The Rotarian,* he arranged for a former student of his at Medill, Roland E. Wolseley, to collaborate by doing a good part of the donkeywork. Wolseley was teaching journalism at Mundelein College on Chicago's northside, and was delighted to be involved. Leland worked out the legal arrangements with Macmillan and Mrs. Bastian's attorney. The revised edition of *Around the Copydesk* was published under the authorship of Bastian Case Wolseley. It gave the young professor a nice line in his resume, so he wrote Leland his thanks for including him in the project.

Despite the pace at which Leland worked, the Cases were able to attend concerts and the theater, of which Chicago had plenty. They sometimes attended the Sunday Evening Club, which presented speakers such as William Lyon Phelps, renowned professor of English at Yale University. The Cases held parties in their home for friends and staff. Josephine was building her concert career, and would often entertain guests by singing. The songs represented national cultures, which she illustrated with costumes from her collection.

Josephine's mother came to live with the Cases in Evanston. Since her name was Josephine Smith Altman, Leland and his bride adopted for Mrs. Leland D. Case the nickname Joan, pronounced "JoAnn," but always, always spelled "Joan."

Leland, as a matter of fact, was always called "Leland"— to his wife, all of his family, and his friends. On extremely rare occasions someone called him "Lee," but not someone who knew him well. The exception to this was Paul Teetor. Beginning with Acacia days at Northwestern University, Paul was a friend and associate for 30 years, who called Leland "Lee". However, Leland preferred, and was called, "Leland."

The Rotary International convention of 1937 was held in Nice, on the French Riviera. Leland attended for *The Rotarian*, revelling in the atmosphere of France once again and practicing his terrible French. Afterward, he slipped off to northern Europe for a quick vacation to Stockholm.

He visited Skansen, the great open-air museum where the arts, crafts and history of all parts of Sweden are represented. He learned that Dr. Arthur Immanuel Hazelius, a generation before, had studied the way in which his native land was wallowing in a sense of inferiority. The attitude was—for music, go to Berlin; for art, Paris is the place. Hazelius brought to Skansen truly Swedish exhibits, such as beautiful old wooden buildings from the provinces, a revival of folk dancing and singing, and handicrafts, which caused a renaissance of the nation's own indigenous culture.

The result was that the people acquired a new respect for and pride in their own accomplishments. And Sweden developed into a proud, distinctive nation. This experience lived with Leland. He thought of ways in which this idea might meet the need in the Dakotas, which had been hit so hard by The Depression and the Dust Bowl.

CHAPTER IV
The Man of the Middle Border

Late in 1937, Morehouse of the Macmillan Company wrote again about *Editing the Day's News*. The book was showing a profit, and another revision would be timely if he would undertake to have it ready for the 1939-40 academic year. The plan again was to reset the type from cover to cover which meant he could rewrite the book to whatever extent he felt necessary. *Around the Copydesk* was ready for revision again too, and the two books could come out together as a working team.

The pace at *The Rotarian* was a killer. Leland worked his people hard, but he worked himself even harder, and everyone knew it. Overtime work by the staff was an ongoing concern for the magazine committee. Of course Leland's activities outside of the magazine never let up either.

In the midst of this kind of whirlwind there came suddenly a flat calm. On New Year's Eve, 1937, Joan and Francis drove Leland southwest of Chicago to the Hines Hospital to enter treatment for tuberculosis. Leland's physician had made a preliminary diagnosis and had ordered an immediate confinement. How long this condition had been developing is a matter of conjecture, for there is nothing in Leland's papers that even suggests he was having trouble. Certainly the way he was living and working betrayed no sign of it.

"What a strange way to spend New Year's Eve," Leland said to himself, after the family had left and he was there alone in the quiet of the ward. He opened a little book of poems by Henry Morton Robinson that the author had sent to him.

That was a Friday. He slept well and read Will Durant's *Story of Philosophy* most of Saturday. It puzzled him why he rushed to spend a quiet New Year weekend in the hospital. He just didn't understand that what he needed most was to do nothing. Sunday Joan visited him, and he wrote four or five letters. An extended rest was the order.

Life at Hines Hospital was not all staring out the window—although he noted in his diary the winter scene outside. He ran *The Rotarian* from that hospital bed. May Aaberg would make the trip out to the hospital weekly or more often. Leland asked the orderly, "You saw her leave at the end of visiting hours, didn't you?" The orderly would let her out of a side exit hours later. Leland wrote an incredible number of letters. Daniel Longwell of Time Inc. had sent Leland the prospectus for *Life* magazine, and he followed the progress of the new publication with detailed interest. T. C. Moorehouse of Macmillan wrote their condolences, and announced that they had a sufficient stock of *Editing the Day's News* to carry them for a couple of years, so they could forget the revision until he was on his feet again.

In June, Joan and Leland journeyed to the Southwest, to Santa Fe, for his recuperation. Joan scouted around and found a nice four-bedroom adobe house on a quiet lane.

Leland slept late, lounged a lot, read much, and did a good bit of thinking. It wasn't until August that he ventured out in public, the occasion being the annual "Poets Round-up" in a lovely Santa Fe home. Playwright Thornton Wilder was the chairman of the event, and he and Leland had a pleasant chat afterward.

A letter from Paul Teetor helped his morale. Paul told him about an impromptu magazine committee meeting in Chicago, where the principle members explored how to help the staff. "If I read correctly," Leland mused, "I shall have an opportunity when I return not only to retain my health but to make *The*

71

Rotarian go places. Paul's letter is literally medicine for me." And that afternoon he started a watercolor out in the patio. Often those afternoons included a siesta, which in itself was revolutionary for him.

As far as the staff at *The Rotarian* was concerned, Leland was running the magazine, down to the last detail, issue by issue. Karl Krueger says of that time, "I mean, run it. By mail and phone he planned everything, approved everything. He was sick, he was in charge, he was heroic. And somehow he got well on it, beating the then still hard-to-beat TB."

Leland was reading and thinking a great deal and sharing his thoughts with some of his friends, particularly Clint Anderson. In those weeks he found himself pondering about Dakota Wesleyan University.

The school was, in generally accepted terms, a university in name only. Founded in 1885 by Methodists, it had never had an enrollment of much more than 700 students. It had only a small selection of courses for post-graduate credit. But it had maintained a strong reputation, and had been accredited by the North Central Association of Colleges continually since 1916. It was a college that the whole region could depend upon for higher education.

Dakota Wesleyan, of course, had already meant a great deal to Leland's family. Being a private Methodist-oriented institution, it stood for the whole spirit of pioneering and nation-building in the Upper Missouri River Valley. This was 1938, remember. The whole country was just beginning to see its way out of the depths of the Great Depression. The Upper Missouri region had been hard, hard hit, especially agriculture. Prolonged drought had played havoc with much of the land.

Ten percent of the population was leaving, particularly the youth, for "greener pastures." Minneapolis, or better still, Chicago, was where the future lay.

In that time in Santa Fe so many things that had flowed through Leland's mind began to congeal around Dakota Wesleyan and its environment, and ways that he could help it. He thought back to the things he had seen in Sweden the year before and the impression the Skansen Museum had made upon him, the clear inspiration of Sweden's indigenous culture as a distinctive value in a world setting.

The result of this musing was that he drafted an amazing document, by hand, and Harold Cooley, whom Leland had gotten to know in Santa Fe, typed it out for him. Hal was a native of Minnesota who had come to the Southwest to work in archaeology and anthropology. The two men became good friends. Hal delivered the typescript—almost a hundred pages— in a wrapper on which he scribbled doggerel-style the legend, "Open—with a silent prayer! Take it easy! Inflammable! Here IT is!"

"IT" outlined the role that Dakota Wesleyan could play in the rebuilding of the region, culturally, spiritually, intellectually, and in morale. "If Wesleyan has a distinctive and useful type of education to offer," Leland wrote, "it will survive handsomely. If it is 'just another' college, lacking verve and color, its future surely is not too sanguine."

He then set out ideas on strengthening the faculty. He suggested adding exchange professors, including some from foreign countries, adding guest lecturers, new courses—the "new" science of anthropology, for example, and architecture—with specific rationale and concepts for each of these proposals. He drew on the visual attractiveness of the place itself. He proceeded with an in-depth study of trends in college education and of the needs of South Dakota. He took a look at other colleges in the state and their strengths and weaknesses. Leland focused on the basic philosophy inherent in the settling of South Dakota—self-reliance and ingenuity, fun, faith, honesty.

There were 20 pages on establishing a cultural center for the Middle Border—referring to author Hamlin Garland's phrase for that whole upper Missouri region comprised basically of North and South Dakota, western Minnesota, and some of the adjacent areas. He envisioned a Dakota Pioneer museum, patterned on the Swedish model with a bow to Henry Ford's Greenfield Village in Dearborn, Michigan and to Colonial Williamsburg in Virginia. He talked of a library, an outdoor theater, WPA financing (Works Progress Administration, a federal government program of the depression era), contributions from the city of Mitchell, plans for endowment, staffing, a board of directors and on and on. It was to be independent of the university but working closely with it. It was a full-fledged concept.

Then—startling to see in the perspective of the following 50 years—Leland offered to come to Mitchell, the home of Dakota Wesleyan, and work to create this institution. He would teach part-time at DWU and help with college public relations to "earn his keep."

He offered to do this, if room and board were provided, for a cash salary of $30 per month. His concept included organizing a "Sod Shanty Press" to produce booklets and publications arising out of the cultural work of the new institution and also job-printing for the university in general; organizing the museum; directing research into the archaeology and history of the region; and organizing and coordinating an extension service involving speakers, musical programs and exhibitions for

74

the surrounding towns, service clubs, conventions and schools. He would start in the spring of 1939 and would expect to contract to work for 18 months. At that time the effort should be evaluated, he proposed, and a new agreement drawn up if they decided to move ahead.

Leland worked on this plan for several months. He shared it with his brother Francis, who backed him strongly and made suggestions about how it might be of most help to Dakota Wesleyan. They referred to it together, and with Hal Cooley, as the Big Idea.

Leland's thinking was crystallized in a meeting with Hamlin Garland who was preparing an article for *The Rotarian*. He stopped off in Santa Fe to visit with Leland. They discussed the idea for Dakota Wesleyan and the region. Garland's response was most encouraging. Leland shared his thinking also with Clinton Anderson, in nearby Albuquerque, who responded wholeheartedly and backed up his enthusiasm for the idea with a check for $100 to help get it off the ground.

When Leland's proposal for a Middle Border cultural enterprise was ready to be presented to Dakota Wesleyan University, Leland asked Hal to go up to Mitchell with it and join Francis Case, who was to make the presentation. Leland himself was paying close attention to his doctor's orders and staying in the Southwest out of action. So, as the minutes of the executive committee meeting of the board of directors of the university read for December 24, 1938, "Congressman Francis Case and Professor Cooley" gave the board a full account of the purpose and necessity for the cultural center.

The presentation led off with one of Leland's favorite quotations, from Chicago architect David Burnham: "Make no little plans, for they have no magic to stir men's blood." It set the proposal before the background of the Spirit of the Pioneers, a distinctive American characteristic, spelled out as—

Self-Reliance—working out one's own problems; using the resources at hand
Originality—new problems require new solutions
Honesty—being what you are in the process of becoming what you want to be.
Optimism—attitude of seeing set-backs as temporary inconveniences only.
Self development—appreciation of the value of education, and striving to get it.

Those points were Leland's credo, and he saw them as the clue to the future of the Upper Missouri Valley and its people.

Lauritz Miller, an attorney in Mitchell, was chairman of the board of Dakota Wesleyan and of its executive committee. Under his direction they set up two committees. One was to study the costs of building the proposed structure, of rammed earth to house an enlarged college library, a pioneer museum, and a modern art gallery with an outdoor theatre next to it; the other committee, to study the plans and purposes of the whole project.

The sojourn in Santa Fe was having its effect upon Leland's health. He accepted the Macmillan Company's request to rework completely *Editing the Day's News*, saying that, "this glorious climate of the Southwest, enormous quantities of food, and unbelievable periods of horizontal rest are putting me back on my feet." Their tentative plan was for the book to be out in 1940.

He pointed out to the Macmillan people that his 1932 revision was as far as he knew, the first journalistic book to fore-cast the importance of photography in current journalism.

By midsummer of 1939, the Cases were back in Chicago, and he was fully in gear again. Getting caught up with things at *The Rotarian* wasn't a problem, for the process ran as if he had never been away. Maybe that was part of the secret—as far as the magazine was concerned, in his own mind, he may never have been out of the office. And his work on the magazine, his development of Friends of the Middle Border, his revision of *Editing the Day's News*, his civic and professional work out-side the office—all rolled steadily ahead. There is little sense that he was a man recovering from a serious bout with TB.

Looking at the editorial needs of his *Rotarian*, Leland reached out to Hal Cooley, who was in Dallas working on a job possibility, and offered him a position as editorial assistant.

Hal stayed about eight months. He was one of many men who worked for Editor Case who—although respecting his qualities as a journalist—just couldn't work under his style of leadership. A host of men like Cooley—some of whom went to the top of their field—came, tried, and left, over the years.

At the same time, for each of these men whom I have come across, Leland himself had appreciation and respect. He would recommend them, even generously, and follow their careers with interest. With Cooley, Leland seemed to have a life-time concern. Maybe, as Cooley says, it was because Leland could talk him into doing anything he suggested.

Leland consulted Dakota Wesleyan and other institutions in the Middle Border region to be sure that DWU was the right anchor for Friends of the Middle Border, and satisfied himself that this was the natural tie-in for what he had in mind. Be-tween efforts at Chicago and at Mitchell, articles of incorporation for the new organization were prepared. Leland assembled a committee of men of the Mitchell community, along with Clinton Anderson and himself, as incorporators. In September, 1940, the corporation was recorded in the office of the Secretary of State of South Dakota.

There was nothing half-baked or parochial about the Board of Directors that Leland assembled for Friends of the Middle Border. Here the widely known editor of *The Rotarian* called upon men whom he had met and worked with while building a magazine of excellence, and they accepted. It was a catalogue of leading Americans who had ties with the Upper Missouri Valley: James Truslow Adams, historian, Chancellor of the American Academy of Arts & Letters; Clinton Anderson, Dakota Wesleyan alumnus, prominent international Rotarian, businessman, politician; Gutzon Borglum, internationally known sculptor, creator of the Mt. Rushmore Memorial; John Dewey, philosopher, educator; Hamlin Garland, author, coiner of the phrase "the Middle Border;" Paul P. Harris, founder of Rotary; and Stewart Edward White, novelist. In addition were eight men of Mitchell and Dakota Wesleyan University, including Joseph Edge, DWU president, along with an alumnus and businessman of Kansas City, and Leland Case of Evanston.

The Big Idea of Friends of the Middle Border was timely for Dakota Wesleyan. Dr. James Van Kirk, professor of history who carried a full load of responsibilities at the college, nevertheless was deeply involved, along with his wife Elizabeth. The energy put into the new enterprise was reflected week by week in the volume of correspondence and telephone calls with Leland Case in Chicago.

An advisory board was put together, that included John Collier, U.S. Commissioner of Indian Affairs for matters anthropological; Frank Lloyd Wright, architect; Grant Wood and John Sloan, artists; and author Carl Sandburg.

And what of Leland's offer to drop everything in Chicago and move to Mitchell to work on Friends of the Middle Border? Perhaps that part of the draft concept was never presented; we may never know. A fire in 1955 destroyed much of the original records at Mitchell, including records of Dakota Wesleyan, as well as of the Friends.

It may well be that Professor Van Kirk, Lauritz Miller, and the others saw the advantage of having Leland in Chicago using his influence around the nation for FMB. We do know that a good chunk of Leland's heart was with the project as long as he lived, and that he gave advice, counsel, talent and treasure to it over the next 46 years. Clearly, to Leland the creation of Friends of the Middle Border was one of the most important elements in his entire life's work.

There was a camaraderie in the offices of *The Rotarian*. It came from the top but was fed by the men and women the editor gathered around him. Leland liked to have every employee come into his office and say goodnight before departing each working day. Why was this? Was it his concern for them as people? Was it his interest in what hours they were putting in? Often a person coming in to say goodnight found herself or himself sitting there an hour later either listening to Leland's stories, or receiving assignments for the next day—or both. The stories were endless and fascinating, for Leland was always in personal touch with much that was making world headlines.

The office spirit played a big part in one of Leland's efforts. In 1940 he was considering a major change in the format of *The Rotarian* and of its Spanish language counterpart, *Revista*

Dr. Walter Head, President of Rotary International, attacking Leland Case (right) in skit designed to make the point that THE ROTARIAN *needed a new format— 1940*

Rotaria. To sell the change, Leland arranged a party at a restaurant in downtown Chicago. He invited the magazine committee, the current president of Rotary International Dr. Walter D. Head of Montclair, New Jersey, and General Secretary Ches Perry—and then he bade the staff create the party.

The staff's labors resulted in an old-fashioned melodrama on the theme of the quest for a format change. It was staged before a homemade paper backdrop and with wild costumes. The cast featured Walter Head in a "Lone Ranger" mask and Indian warbonnet attacking a determined Cowboy Case with a dinner fork. The drama included the mellifluous singing of a Spanish-style duet by Joan Case and Ida Hinojosa. May Aaberg represented a sorrowing Rejection Slip, weeping gently into a handkerchief. The party was a smashing success. The editor got his new format.

In revising *Editing the Day's News*, Leland took time to rethink the purpose of the book. He felt that journalism-as-taught should go more deeply into psychology than did the rule-of-thumb journalism learned by practice. He devoted an entire chapter to those social considerations a good newspaperman should take into account in selecting material for his columns. "'It happened' is the only reason some newspapermen think counts", he wrote, "but without losing news values, I try to point out that 'the way the story is presented' may give it social values too. If I succeed, the book's emphasis will not be the less on the practical aspect of newspapering, but will inject into it the 'public weal' note so frequently glossed over or entirely ignored." To his knowledge, he was dealing with this aspect of journalism more thoroughly than any book in the field.

The student newspaper at Dakota Wesleyan University played a big role in promoting Friends of the Middle Border. The paper, *The Phreno Cosmian*, was named in 1890 for the first literary society formed on campus. At Thanksgiving, 1940, the paper carried a front-page feature story with banner headline "Ideals of Leland Case Materialize. Promotion of Interest in Middle Border Culture is Aim of FMB."

"Leland D. Case, ex-22 and editor of *The Rotarian*," the story read, "has been the founder and chief source of inspiration of Friends of the Middle Border. The main collection, art, libraries, and social history museum now has three rooms in

81

Science Hall, while the music collection is housed in the School of Music. It would seem that the time is not far distant when the dream of having a rammed-earth building, to symbolize the sod house of the pioneer, with a log wing, symbolizing the prospector's cabin, should become a reality. In this combination art gallery, library, and museum would be rooms where the various clubs of the campus and community could meet. For Friends of the Middle Border collections are not cold museum collections, but materials that the people of the Middle Border work with and use."

This ferment of interest and the gathering of materials and artifacts had all come about within the year. Dr. Van Kirk and his wife became a focus for the interest, he as supervising director, she as editor of the new *Middle Border Bulletin*. Lauritz Miller was active, and Dr. J. Almus Russell, Director of the English Department became curator of the Middle Border library of rare books and manuscripts. Matthew D. Smith, dean and later president, responded wholeheartedly to the research and documentary side of the plan. He was a great-nephew of Jedediah Smith, who had been such a powerful figure in the opening of this great land. The whole school was involved in key events, such as the unveiling of a portrait of Jedediah Smith, during a chapel service. Leland Case and other supporters in Chicago had commissioned the painting and sent it to the campus for the Friends. Dr. Russell donated a number of rare and valuable books.

"To say that FMB is an asset to Dakota Wesleyan would be a gross understatement," *The Phreno Cosmian* said a few months later.

Forever after, Leland would point to the fact that the Dakota Art Gallery at Friends of the Middle Border was the first public art collection in the Dakotas.

James Truslow Adams turned out to be one of the most important elements in this development. From his home in Connecticut, and with his vital connections to the foremost artists and writers of the land, he promoted Friends of the Middle Border as one of the finest examples of The American Dream— one of his great concepts in America's story. As Chancellor of the American Academy of Arts and Letters he drafted a statement about the young prairie entity at Mitchell and sent it to the 50 members of the Academy and the 250 members of the Institute of Arts and Letters, of which the Academy represented the cream.

From that action flowed gifts of literary and art works from the membership to FMB, including a fine painting by Childe Hassam, one of the foremost American painters of the period. Works from this group continued to come to FMB for years after that. Case, 25 years younger than Adams, had great respect for him. The relationship progressed slowly from "Dr. Adams" and "Mr. Case" to "Jim" and "Leland" by the time Adams died in 1949. After that, Leland and Joan kept in touch with Kay, his widow, through letters and visits.

Promoting the natural ties to Friends of the Middle Border was a strong note in Leland's thinking. Chief among these was the renowned American sculptor James Earle Fraser. When Fraser was four years old his father, a railroad engineer, moved his family to Mitchell to develop the Milwaukee line through the town and north to Aberdeen. James learned to carve in the soft native chalkstone that hardened gradually when exposed to the air. An experience that stayed with Fraser all his life was watching an old Sioux medicine man praying to the four points of the compass for the return of the buffalo to his people.

The memory of that Indian mingled in his mind with the words of an old plainsman who visited with the family—that the progress of the white man across the land would result in the Indian being pushed all the way to the Pacific ocean, and that would be the end of his trail. At the age of 15 James created the first version of the now—famous piece that bore that name. In 1915 he was commissioned to do a larger-than-life version of *The End of the Trail* for the Panama-Pacific Exposition in San Francisco. Fraser went on to create important pieces in many cities of the United States and, with his wife Laura Gardin Fraser, was responsible for some of America's best-known works—the most widely recognized of which is the Indian-head nickel.

Acquiring for Friends of the Middle Border a version of *The End of the Trail* was one of Leland's great ambitions. He talked with Fraser about it—Mitchell was the birthplace of the statue, and here a major representation of it surely belonged. Fraser responded, but to have the ambition was not necessarily to achieve the reality. It was 40 years before *The End of the Trail* came home to Mitchell.

A senior majoring in art named Dean Nauman was among the many students at Dakota Wesleyan who took a special interest in Friends of the Middle Border. Dr. Van Kirk and the others hired Nauman to stay on after his graduation and be the executive secretary of the new organization. They found work to support him, including that of teaching assistant in art. Dean had already agreed to paint a mural of Jedediah Smith to become part of the Friends collection, and given as a gift from his graduating class.

Dean had a well rounded talent. In addition to coping with the paintings, prints, books, artifacts, and manuscripts that were flowing in, he had to create displays and scrounge for materials. He had a sense of public relations in the community, as well as the knack of getting along with the kaleidoscope of personalities involved. He understood the grand work of creating a regional self-consciousness, of personal contact with those who had pride in the region, and who could aid the work financially.

Dean realized the importance of Leland Case, in far-off Chicago, and the resources Case was bringing to bear from his vantage point at *The Rotarian*. He eagerly took direction from Case, who would give him names of people to contact about FMB and the progress there, and how to ask for things to benefit the fledgling institution.

Symbolic of how vital and integral the Friends of the Middle Border was to the life of Dakota Wesleyan University was the persistent treatment of it in *The Phreno Cosmian*. The paper chronicled gifts that were given to FMB, speeches made under its auspices, and cultural programs that it presented. It outlined the origin of the Middle Border concept: in 1849, following the discovery of gold in California, a great migration surged westward and settled in the far West; in the late '70s and early '80s, following the discovery of gold in the Black Hills by General Custer's expedition in 1874, another influx of settlers moved westward into that area; then the 49ers from California surged back eastward, and the two waves of humanity—all in search of gold—came together along the upper Missouri.

"This region became the middle border—the point of contact. These hardy westerners represented all walks of life. Some were adventurers. Others were literary people—trained in eastern schools. All were in search of the New Eldorado. After a half century, they left behind them many valuable books, maps, historical documents, weapons of defense and offense, and other pioneer relics. It has now become the voluntary task of the Friends of the Middle Border to collect all of this material and to care for it at Dakota Wesleyan, until such time as a separate building can be erected in which to house it. It is rapidly developing Dakota Wesleyan into a cultural center."

Leland managed to get to Mitchell from time to time. At commencement in 1941 he was awarded the honorary Doctor of Letters, the first of his half-dozen honorary degrees. In the fall of that year he attended a memorial service at the Dakota Wesleyan Chapel, at which the Jedediah Smith mural Dean Nauman painted was presented. The importance of the painting to Dakota Wesleyan was that the incident it portrayed— Jed Smith offering a prayer on the bank of the Missouri River— was the first known instance of an event of a religious character in the white man's world west of the river.

Work at *The Rotarian* was able to bring so many of Leland's interests together. Artist Charles Hargens, who had been born and raised in Hot Springs in the Black Hills, illustrated articles for Leland from time to time, and was also becoming interested in Friends of the Middle Border. James Truslow Adams contributed articles regularly to *The Rotarian*. Friends of the Middle Border, infused as it was with what were seen as the basic virtues of the American character—self-reliance, conviction, independance, willingness to work hard—were the stuff of Adams's great concept of The American Dream.

Leland thought of these people as friends—colleagues, potential or actual contributors one way or another—but friends. Charles Hargens outlived him, staunchly a friend. Adams maintained a warm relationship until he died. James Earle Fraser

Leland and Joan at their home in Evanston, about 1940

and his wife became closer friends with Leland as time went on. The men at *Readers Digest*—De Witt Wallace and Charles Ferguson—friends for life.

The Case family helped with FMB. His father, Herbert, in Mankato, wrote letters and visited people who might give family memorabilia and documents to the collection. His sisters were on the lookout for things. His brother in Congress, whose ties to Dakota Wesleyan were even stronger than were Leland's, turned up many items of value for the museum and the collections. Francis and Leland, in letters and conversations, used the symbol BI for the Big Idea. As time went along, they referred to BI as the Bigger Idea. When they got really excited they referred to BABI—Bigger And Better Idea.

In the midst of a busy career there were good touches of home life for Joan and Leland. They enjoyed reading together. They read *The Education of Henry Adams*, with its foreword by their new friend James Truslow Adams, and then they got into Adams's own major work *Epic of America*. Joan had her singing career—she stopped teaching a few years after they were married—and she did professional concerts with her costume collection embellishing her music.

The problems of the Great Depression had given way to issues facing a world at war. World War II had engulfed much of Europe and Asia and had drawn most of the civilized world with it. The United States, while mainly in total sympathy with the Allied powers, was "isolationist." Leland and Ches Perry discussed at length the editorial posture that was proper for *The Rotarian*, official magazine of Rotary International. There were member clubs, after all, in every developed country of the world including Germany, Italy and Japan—although this quandary had been made much easier by the Nazi party ordering its members to resign from Rotary.

Walter Head, after his year as Rotary president, accepted to chair a "Committee on Research as to Participation of Rotarians in Post War World Reorganization." Thinking for this proposition, and how *The Rotarian* could promote it, was the kind of challenge Leland loved. It made up in part for his ineligibility for military service, which was based on his history of tuberculosis.

Leland generated a series of articles to stimulate thinking among Rotarians on the problem of creating a stable world at the war's end. He also produced a volume for publication by

Rotary International which he called *A World to Live In*. For the book he collected a group of articles from *The Rotarian* that he felt would picture the world as it should be after the struggle against the Axis powers. It appeared in 1942. In 1944 he edited a similar volume called *Peace is a Process*, and a third in 1946, *Peace Requires Action*.

Meanwhile, Leland was developing support for Friends of the Middle Border among the Dakota Wesleyan alumni of the Chicago area. He and his friend Elmo Scott Watson put their heads together and established a Chicago chapter of FMB. They thought this would be but the first of many FMB chapters around the country. They made lists of potential members and began a recruiting effort. They divided the Chicago chapter work into interest groups: literature, art, and history. Elmo worked particularly hard on the latter group.

Two men on the staff of the *Chicago Daily News* at the time were Don Russell, City Editor, and Herman Gastrell Seely, financial writer, who were friends of Watson's. Seely and his brother-in-law, named Dr. Will Frackleton from Wyoming, had earlier collaborated on a book entitled *Sagebrush Dentist*. Watson and Case decided it would be a good idea to get some of their FMB contacts together, and the occasion they settled on was to hear "Doc" Frackleton spin some yarns from his book. The group they corralled to meet him turned out to be genuinely interested in meeting for similar programs and in sharing their love of Western lore.

Eleven of them met at the Watson home in Evanston in late December of 1942. Don Russell thought it was just too cold to go out. Seely didn't make it either. From this point the building of a membership for a Friends of the Middle Border chapter continued, and for several years there were annual banquets with distinguished speakers.

The war took Dean Nauman into service and away from Friends of the Middle Border. Leland lost the invaluable services of May Aaberg at that time. She bade farewell to her friends and her life in Chicago and enlisted in the WAC—the Womens' Army Corps. Over the next several years she dropped in sometimes at *The Rotarian* offices, trim in her uniform.

After the war May worked for the federal government in the occupation and rebuilding of Japan and Germany. When she returned, Francis Case asked her to be his secretary in Washington, and the rest of her working life has been spent there.

The war effort also swept up Leland's sister Carol. Carol had married an attorney from Hot Springs, Bertin Goddard. Goddard was an outdoorsman and hunter. Carol liked to say that he had been attracted to her because she could shoot so well. Goddard had been born with a deformed foot. Unable to serve himself, he encouraged Carol to enlist in the WAC, and she served as an administrator for the Army Air Corps at Rapid City and at Fort Sheridan. In her spare time, she presented plays for the troops.

The new edition of *Editing the Day's News* was published early in 1943. The comment of Mitchell Carney, managing editor of *Journalism Quarterly* and professor of journalism at the University of Minnesota, made all the effort seem worthwhile: "My guess is that it will push everything else out of the picture. I am greatly impressed by the fact that, in a book that necessarily deals largely with tools and techniques, you've done so much to keep the student aware that the newspaper is a social instrument and that it bears heavy social responsibility—and you've done magnificently with the primary job as well."

Leland's work on *The Rotarian* produced one particular historical footnote—and a good article for the magazine. Leland heard by some informal grapevine that a woman in Philadelphia had information on the origin of the movement that led to "The Star Spangled Banner" becoming America's national anthem. He managed to reach her and got the story.

It seems that at Fort Meade, a location vivid in the memories of Leland's childhood, the bandmaster had taken the Francis Scott Key piece to his heart and had played it frequently. The post commandant, Colonel Caleb Carlton of the Eighth Cavalry, had discussed with his wife the need for a national air and they decided this was it. He ordered that it be played at retreat and at the close of parades and concerts. Before long this stirring march was picked up by others and became widely known. The Secretary of War, Daniel Lamont, decreed it a must for all army installations. In 1931 Congress adopted it as our national anthem.

Leland's interest in language sometimes caused repercussions around the editorial offices of *The Rotarian*. One day a project he had assigned failed to mature. Leland said—well, he guessed it had fallen between the stools. What in the world did that mean? Leland explained that out in the great wheat lands of the Dakotas, the wheat stalks were known as stools. While harvesting they tried to let as little grain as possible "fall between the stools." Illustrations like this stuck with his staff for life.

The phrase of Leland's that lingered longest in the minds of his staff was "The Desideratum." One day they were discussing with the chief the subject of overtime, asking about the many evening hours and weekends that they were working.

Leland promised that when they reached "the desideratum," then overtime would dwindle perhaps to nothing.

Years later Karl Krueger told me about the phrase: "Anyone would know the meaning of the big word even if he had flunked Latin I, but the word itself—so formidable! Back there in our workroom 'The Desideratum' was always good for a smile, but we never reached the one Leland had in mind. Perhaps now that he has passed on from this life he will have reached 'The Desideratum.'"

From the offices of Rotary on Wacker Drive, Leland used a good number of his lunch hours to prowl the bookstores in the Loop, often with one of his pals. This lunchtime practice became a feature for him through his years in Chicago. He particularly collected first editions, whenever he could, and if the author were still living, he would map a campaign to have the book autographed.

CHAPTER V
The Westerners

January 30, 1944—Leland, Elmo Watson and Paul Kieser met in the Case "kiva," Leland's study at his home in Evanston. Kieser was a colleague of Leland's at Rotary International and a book collector. The three men had been part of the group who had gathered to hear the Wyoming dentist spin his yarns some 13 months before. They were meeting to pursue something that Elmo had sensed that night, that the focus of interest had gone beyond Friends of the Middle Border. There was a devotion to western history and lore amoung the men that ran wide and deep. Elmo, Paul and Leland knew they were on to something. The impulse that had initiated Friends of the Middle Border was about to give birth to something much wider.

The three men called a meeting, which they foresaw as the first of a series of monthly "round-ups." On February 25, 1944, a cold and wintry evening, 14 men gathered at the home the Watsons had moved to in Winnetka at 824 Prospect Street. Clarence Paine, librarian at Beloit College in Wisconsin, made the trip to present a "short and unlearned treatise on Calamity Jane." Most of the men in the group did not know each other personally, but many were familiar to each other by their reputations as scholars, formally or informally, on the great subject of the West.

Present were five of the men who had met in December of 1942: Arthur Dailey, advertising manager of the Santa Fe Railroad; Leland; Kieser; Clarence Paine; and Watson, of course. Also present was Everett D. Graff, president of the Ryerson Steel Company and a collector of Western Americana, who had a great interest in the Newberry Library in Chicago; Marc

Elmo Scott Watson (courtesy of Northwestern University archives)

Green, editor of *The Milwaukee Railway Magazine*; Fred B. Hackett, elevator engineer who had travelled both with Buffalo Bill and with the 101 RanchWild West Show; Mannel Hahn, part of the research staff of *The Rotarian*, one of the founders of the Burlington, Wisconsin, Historical Society, and who claimed to be the inventor of the Burlington Liars Club; Franklin J. Meine, editor for Consolidated Book Publishers, Inc. and authority on tall tales and frontier humor; the poet John G. Neihardt, chief of information for the U.S. Indian Service and who was at work on his narrative epic *A Cycle of the West* (the Indian Service was one of the branches of the U.S. government that was moved from Washington during the war and housed in the Merchandise Mart in Chicago); Don Russell and his workmate Herman Seely; and Burleigh Withers, artist and

94

advertising illustrator. Another man tagged along with one of the group but had no interest in the evening. His name has drifted off into oblivion.

After Paine's talk, the group sat together to yarn about related topics, and discuss what they should do next and whether to organize themselves. And someone—nobody could ever remember who—said, "Why not call ourselves the Westerners?"

This was the beginning of an outfit that today has over 100 chapters in 13 countries, with about 5000 members.

In the minds of Watson and Case, this success was a direct result of their interest in Friends of the Middle Border, and each remained loyal to both concepts.

Elmo was appointed "Sheriff" of the "Posse" of the new group—that is, the executive committee to run the show, with Leland and Franklin Meine as "Deputies." The Posse's charge was to determine the minimum of machinery needed to keep the group in operation.

The next meeting, held in Chicago in March at the Cliff Dwellers Club (founded in 1905 by Hamlin Garland), approved the suggestions made by the Posse. It was a dinner meeting, which ended with the group gathered in comfortable chairs around the big fireplace for an informal talk. The yarn-spinner was their own Don Russell, who spoke in an easy-going style concerning the research he was doing to separate myth from fact about that most famous of western outlaws—Jesse James.

The Posse proposed a limit of 50 on regular, resident membership, and a few months later felt compelled to raise that to 75. They proposed annual dues, set at $5 a head, and allocated a dollar of each fee for Mitchell to use in maintaining the tie with Friends of the Middle Border and enrolling the members as subscribers to *The Middle Border Bulletin*. Paine's talk on Calamity Jane and Don Russell's on Jesse James were mimeographed for circulation to the members as *The Westerners Brand Book*. Elmo Scott Watson served as editor. The *Brand Book* was immediately in great demand, so it was decided to accept "corresponding members" whose sole benefit was as subscribers. No limit was set on the number of corresponding members, and libraries were already clamoring for copies of the *Brand Book*.

Watson wrote to Friends of the Middle Border at Mitchell in June to nominate 33 people as new members of The Westerners, including now-Congressman Clinton Anderson of New Mexico, and Harold Cooley, who was serving as a lieutenant in the army. All 33 were to be enrolled as members of FMB for the year and to receive the fall issue of the *Middle Border Bulletin*, which they undertook to sponsor through their dues. Leland sent Elmo a list of 250 names as potential corresponding members in the Westerners and FMB.

Two years later the Chicago group decided to print the *Brand Book* instead of just mimeographing it, raising the question of organizing legally for this publishing venture. Seymour J. Frank, a charter member, was an attorney whose idea of recreation was reading back-issues of the *Congressional Record*. He devised a constitution that was almost no constitution at all. It did not mention a quorum, so the group could do almost anything, at any time, in any way—legally creating a lawless and unorganized institution, which was just the way the Westerners wanted it. As a matter of fact, word got around that everything about this outfit was easy-going and informal, "riding with a loose rein," Leland liked to say, except the *Brand Book*, which maintained a high standard as a publication.

Several characteristics of The Westerners as it evolved over the next years were evident in these first meetings. First was a good meal and comradeship. Second, each meeting involved a good, well-prepared talk on a subject of the West by a speaker who must really know his stuff because several in his audience likely would know aspects of it as as well as he did, if not better. It also helped if the speaker did not take himself too seriously. Although the group would respect the expertise of the speaker, they had no compunctions about entering into lively debate, even a bit of heckling if the mood were right. Thus the tone was set for an informal organization that left business affairs to the Posse so the members could concentrate on fellowship and the subject at hand.

Don Russell, who for over 40 years was one of the Chicago Westerners' mainstays, liked to say that business meetings of the Posse were brief—one fellow missed an entire meeting while hanging up his coat—and that one of their annual meetings was clocked at two minutes, 39 seconds, including a recess.

The Westerners was such a great idea for men with an interest in western lore and history that the members saw the value of spreading the word. Leland made frequent trips out of town, so he used his visits to other cities to do a bit of missionary work, followed up with correspondence. His first efforts were in New York, Washington, Los Angeles, San Francisco, and Denver. The result in Denver was immediate. "The reaction was generally favorable," Leland wrote later, "but some doubts were expressed that Denverites, being in what they conceded was the heart of the West, should be 'No. 2' to an organization in effete Chicago, which was linked with a headquarters at the 'eastern' city of Mitchell, South Dakota."

Leland relayed this particular line of objection to the Posse in Chicago, and it was agreed that the tie to Friends of the Middle Border, while appropriate for the Chicago group, was not a necessary prerequisite for Denver.

In no time, the question arose concerning the need for some sort of national organization. Paul Friggens, a friend of Leland's who had been born on a farm in St. Onge, South Dakota, was working for the Associated Press and living in Tenefly, New Jersey. He had been thinking about establishing a Friends of the Middle Border chapter for New York. Leland gave him background on what had been done in Chicago and also told him about The Westerners. They agreed that a network was needed for the interchange of information, gossip and news, particularly if it served to connect men who were looking for facts on topics they were studying. The Chicago crowd were beginning to see their *Brand Book* as a means of communication and began to print some of the letters they received from around the country.

But beyond talk of exchanging publications or of having corresponding members, as Leland said in a letter to Denver late in 1944, "In fact, we took no action to set up a 'national' Westerners organization which conceivably might have headquarters in Chicago. Rather, we left the side doors open for the wind to sweep across the stage. I'm making carbons for the other Posse members so they'll be posted on what I've said and correct me if I haven't mirrored the results of our powwow."

Leland discussed all of these aspects with Paul Friggens. He mentioned that The Westerners had been set up for men, but Friends of the Middle Border was open to both men and women, and that made it of greater interest for some.

Through the years, Leland took part in meetings of the Chicago Westerners and undoubtedly made many contributions, but the Chicago *Brand Book* shows no mention that he presented a paper. He was one of a four-man panel discussion on

98

The Westerners

Custer's Last Stand for the Chicago group in October 1944. Of the four, only Don Russell and Herman Seeley submitted their notes for publication. Leland provided an outline of Custer's campaign and distributed copies of the P.W. Norris map of 1877. John Jameson, the fourth panel member, showed photos of the battle terrain and discussed whether or not Custer had disobeyed orders.

Leland sent the Chicago group's *Brand Book* to all sorts of people. James Truslow Adams responded with real interest in the material the monthly editions contained. This, even in the first year, was a bellwether of what was to come for The Westerners. Scholars like Adams and libraries all over the country were taking note that these men, so many of them laymen with a passionate avocation for western history, were producing relevant material documenting not only the history and culture of the West, but also of the American experience. It was a new factor to be considered by historians—here was source material, often fresh, often developed by the nonprofessional.

In Washington, Francis Case was involved from the Congressional end with setting up a conference of the free nations of the world in San Francisco, that would try to develop a new world organization. The League of Nations had died with the Italian invasion of Ethiopia and the events of World War II. Francis arranged for Leland to be included in the American delegation as associate consultant to the State Department. Leland spent several months in San Francisco during the spring of 1945. He lived at the Bohemian Club. In addition to the delegates, there were 1800 representatives from newspapers and radio stations around the world. As the work of the conference unfolded in the form of The United Nations Organization, Francis led a bid for the establishment of its headquarters in the Black Hills.

The deliberations in San Francisco concerned ideas that Rotary and *The Rotarian* had been discussing all during the war. Never before in world history had nations met to plan peace, even as war was hotly proceeding. Rotary's leadership took seriously the task of keeping its membership informed about the progress of the conference and, following it, the progress of the young United Nations. The magazine maintained this effort, building, informing, and creating a constituency for a world that works together—as compared to the strong bent toward isolation that had characterized the thinking of many Americans before the war.

When his duties at the conference permitted, Leland took time to get better acquainted with Stewart Edward White, who was living in nearby Burlingame. White was one of the incorporators of Friends of the Middle Border. His novels, many of them about the West, had been appearing since 1901. Actually, the name "The Westerners" had first appeared as the title of one of his novels, and Leland was inclined to believe that that was where the Chicago group had gotten the name. The visit was timed providentially, because within the year White died.

At the end of the war, the mustering-out of America's huge wartime armed forces meant that the short-handed conditions under which *The Rotarian* had operated during the war were beginning to ease. As Leland wrote to his friend Charles Ferguson, now with the United States Information Services in London, "Perhaps some of us who haven't been doing very much of it will now have an opportunity of getting in a bit of home life again."

The Westerners

One of the men Leland recruited for *The Rotarian* during this time was Donald W. Sigler. Don was a dour Nebraskan who had studied journalism at the university there, and like many in that day, had learned much of his craft from *Editing the Day's News*. In addition to being an able writer, he was a fine photographer. Leland was keen on photography for the magazine, yet *The Rotarian* had no darkroom. Don improvised one in the basement of the duplex where he and his wife Lyda lived, and he processed many of the most important shots that appeared in print, such as the ones Leland took on his visit with Albert Einstein.

Don was a much more relaxed person than the boss was. One day Leland was going over Don's copy with his now-legendary purple pen, while Don gazed out the window at the river. Up the river came a captured German submarine, truly not a usual sight for inland Chicago, on its way to the Museum of Science & Industry. Don called his chief's attention to this great event, but Leland never even looked up from the copy.

Most of the feature articles in *The Rotarian* were solicited by the editor himself—90 percent of them, in fact. Leland kept up a huge correspondence with the key people in every field of interest as a way of feeding the magazine with material. This alone was a full-time job. Sometimes it took years to arrange for a story. For example, Robert A. Millikan, Nobel Prize winner for Physics at the California Institute of Technology, declined in 1935 and again in 1939, saying he was just too busy. Finally, Leland and his crew drafted an article drawn from several of Dr. Millikan's speeches and papers and sent it to him asking to publish it in the magazine. At first Millikan declined, then he reread the article, decided it was fine, and authorized its publication over his signature.

101

In addition to the pieces solicited for the magazine and to the material that the staff created itself during the mid-'40s, a flow of about 300 unsolicited stories a month was received at the office from writers all over the world who wanted to be published in *The Rotarian*.

One of Leland's most satisfying personal interviews was with Orville Wright, the surviving one of the famous Wright brothers, the first human beings to fly successfully in a powered heavier-than-air machine. His brother Wilbur Wright had died in 1912 of typhoid fever. Orville Wright was an honorary member of the Rotary Club of Dayton, Ohio. A fellow member helped Leland make contact with him. Leland flew to Dayton in a Lockheed Constellation, whose wing-spread, Leland liked to say, was three feet wider than the 120-foot first flight the Wright brothers had made in 1903. They talked in the modest brick shop where Wright worked. Leland asked him whether he and his brother had expected their pioneering to grow into aviation as it was now. "Not at all," he replied. "We did it for fun." "Not to make money?" "No, at one time we could have sold out for very little—VERY little. If our first interest really had been money, we would have tried something in which the chances for success were much brighter!"

The conversation went beautifully, until Leland, suddenly realizing he was going to be late for another appointment, decided to call a taxi. Wright was extremely apologetic for keeping him so long, and insisted on taking him to the appointment in his own ancient Hudson. Leland was the last man to interview Wright; a few weeks later, Orville Wright was dead.

For some time Leland had been thinking about creating a guide book to the Black Hills. In his many European trips he had used the Baedeker books with their wealth of detail; in Paris, for instance, they listed such places as the spot where an assasin had leapt into the carriage of Henry IV and stabbed him to death, or the rooming house where the ambitious Napoleon Bonaparte had stayed when he first came to the city. Leland knew that a really well-researched book on the Black Hills would be a boost to the region. In September Joan and he took a vacation tour of South Dakota by car. They spent a memorable day with his old playmate from the claim near Bear Butte, Amos Bovee and his wife Mickey, and on a rambling walk through the countryside, Leland talked about the book. Bovee was interested and offered to help.

The word spread through South Dakota that Leland was collecting materials and anecdotes. His niece, Lois Wilson, reported how children in Hot Springs made a little money by selling cockleburrs to tourists as porcupine eggs. There was the story of Franklin Delano Roosevelt visiting Mt. Rushmore with the sculptor Gutzon Borglum, contemplating the four great historic faces there and asking, "Is there room for another?" Borglum is said to have smiled and replied, "It wasn't planned that way. There's no stone left."

In early 1947 Leland made a business trip by train to San Francisco and Los Angeles. On the *Super Chief*, Leland noticed a youngster named Johnny, whose mother and father were becoming fed up with his energy in those confined circumstances. Learning that Johnny had a birthday the next day, Leland and the Pullman steward teamed up and wired ahead for a birthday cake. At Gallup, New Mexico, they arranged for the conductor to hold the train while they collected the cake, candles, some toys, and wrapping paper. That evening they gathered the other kids on the train into the diner, turned off the lights, and brought in the cake, while singing "Happy Birthday."

Leland had developed a friendship with artist Harvey Dunn. Dunn was a Dakota boy from Manchester who had studied art at the state college in Brookings and had become a prominent artist and illustrator. Leland called upon him several times in his studio at Tenefly, New Jersey, and had talked with him about giving something representative of his work to Friends of the Middle Border.

On one week-end of a Rotary trip he was Dunn's overnight guest. Dunn told him to go alone to his studio where some 40 paintings had been arranged for him to view. Dunn instructed Leland to select one for Friends of the Middle Border. Leland selected *Dakota Woman*. It was shipped to Mitchell, where a ceremony was arranged for its reception. Dunn's sister made the presentation for him. The school band played an original arrangement of three pioneer tunes, all dedicated to Leland Case and FMB.

The idea took root in Dunn's mind that most of his paintings should go back to his home territory in South Dakota, so Leland talked with him about making FMB the repository for his work. By mid-1947 Dunn learned that he had not long to live. He loaded his station wagon with the paintings and drove to Mitchell by himself. Arriving at the Dakota Wesleyan campus, he asked where he would find the art gallery. "Oh, you mean that junk up there on the third floor," a student replied. This made Dunn wonder whether the campus was the right place for his art.

He found his way to the business office, where Gordon Rollins was the new business manager. Dunn asked Rollins if there was a fireproof facility in which to house his paintings if he were to turn them over to FMB. Rollins had no idea that this was a moment of desperation for the artist, and that he was speaking of a load of paintings right outside in the parking lot. Rollins was truthful and replied that, no, at the moment they really didn't have adequate fireproof facilities for the paintings.

Ever since, Gordon Rollins has thought again and again what he might have done differently at that moment; for Harvey Dunn turned away from Dakota Wesleyan and Friends of the Middle Border. He drove north to South Dakota State College in Brookings, where he had received his original art training. Someone there had the quickness of mind and the imagination to give him a real welcome, to tell him they would be thrilled to accept his paintings, and to assure him that they would have a proper home. The college mobilized the South Dakota Federation of Women's Clubs, who mounted a fund drive over the next few years that funded a fine building to house the Harvey Dunn Collection. That, as the saying goes, is history.

In the spring of 1947 Leland and Joan journeyed to Minnesota and South Dakota. They visited Leland's parents. They breakfasted with Dr. Sam Hilburn, new president of Dakota Wesleyan, and his wife, so that Leland could talk with Hilburn about Friends of the Middle Border and its importance to the university. The couple went to the old claim near Bear Butte in Sturgis, and visited with Ezra Bovee, now 80 years old but sharp as ever. That night they were guests at the twenty-fifth anniversary of the Rotary Club in Rapid City; Leland was the speaker and 250 people attended. Next day, at Francis's request and with much feeling, they put flowers on the grave of Francis and Myrle's infant son, who was buried in Mountain View Cemetery.

THE MAN FROM THE HILLS

At the end of May, a Silver Anniversary Dinner was held in the Gold Room of Chicago's Congress Hotel to honor the Medill School of Journalism of Northwestern University. Leland had helped to plan the dinner, dig up missing grads for the invitation list, and write a tribute to the school's work for the dinner program. His piece was titled "A Quarter Century of Service to the Press," and Leland wrote:

"Joseph Medill, distinguished early editor of the *Chicago Tribune*, never attended a school of journalism. There was none in his day....The old movie version of the newspaper man is disappearing. His place is being taken by young men and women who not only know how to write but who have sufficient background in the social sciences to recognize the significance of current events and the ability to interpret them to readers or listeners. These young men and women must recognize their social responsibilitiy to aid the public in forming intelligent opinion and wise judgements...Medill's first quarter century augurs favorably for continued service in supplying the well-trained men and women whom journalism will need in the pivotal period the nation is entering."

The idea of a guidebook to the Black Hills caught the interest of the Black Hills & Badlands Association, a tourism and promotion organization in Sturgis, which lined up a printer in Rapid City. But as 1948 began, Leland was having to ration his time among the April Rotary assembly in Quebec (Rotary's gathering of district governors from around the world for training and up-dating), the Rotary International convention in June in Rio de Janerio, his contribution to a book on the Black Hills for Vanguard Press, and, of course, his monthly *Rotarian* deadlines.

The Westerners

During the convention in Rio, Leland had his first really good look at Latin America—"amused, amazed and impressed by what I saw." Then he took a DC-3 at almost tree-top altitude across the Andes to visit Bolivia and Peru, including a horseback trek to Machu Picchu, "that fantastic Inca stronghold hidden some fifty miles northwest of Cuzco."

That winter Leland visited with James Earle Fraser and his wife Laura at their studio in Westport, Connecticut. Fraser was very pleased with what Leland had to tell him about Friends of the Middle Border: how Harvey Dunn was planning to make some more paintings available, and what James Truslow Adams and the American Academy of Arts & Letters were doing to develop the collections. Fraser spoke in very positive terms about his own part: "I could of course contribute quite a number of pieces along with *The End of the Trail,*" he said. "Should it become possible to use a version of *The End of the Trail* full-sized at Mitchell, I will do everything I can to make it reasonable, for you know I am enthusiastic about anything that can be done for South Dakota."

This kicked off a flurry of activity. Leland drew up a memo for Friends of the Middle Border entitled "An Extraordinary and Urgent Opportunity," a fund- raising effort to build an initial unit of what was to become a complete complex for FMB. He cited the gift of a full city block by Dakota Wesleyan University; architectural services donated by a Chicago man; a log cabin offered by a former South Dakota governor; native-born South Dakotan Robert Pennington, an ex-GI just finishing a PhD and about to become FMB's executive secretary; James Earle Fraser's offer of a 16-inch plaster original of *End of the Trail*; and Harvey Dunn offering "a representative collection" as soon as a fireproof building was completed.

"FMB's art gallery is said to be the only one north of Omaha and west of Minneapolis," Leland said. It would become one of the most important regional collections in America and a fine tourist attraction. Clint Anderson had already donated $1000, to be matched by two other donors. The Chicago chapter convinced a professional fund-raiser to contribute a plan for the campaign.

In the past few years Leland had thought a good bit about one of the Black Hills' early attempts at higher education. In 1887, two years after Dakota Wesleyan had been founded, the citizens of Hot springs with help from the Methodist Church, had started Black Hills College. It folded in 1900. Leland felt that the graduates of Black Hills College, among whom were some very substantial citizens, should have a living link with their deceased alma mater and that such a link could generate loyalty and financial support for Dakota Wesleyan University. He proposed that the university assume the charter of Black Hills College, which had been founded "in perpetuity," and plan events at Dakota Wesleyan to make the alumni feel included on the campus of their sister Methodist institution.

Leland took a very practical step toward this goal. He recieved permission from the Dakota Wesleyan president to arrange for a veteran stone mason from the Black Hills, Henry Berring, to bring a load of Black Hills stone and build a pair of gateposts at the most prominent entrance to Dakota Wesleyan.These were to serve as a memorial to Black Hills College. The dedication of the gateposts and the tie to Black Hills College was duly announced in the February, 1949, alumni issue of the *Dakota Wesleyan University Bulletin*. Scholarship monies began to accumulate in a special fund designated for students from the Hills. The gateposts stand today as a very nice entry point to the campus of Dakota Wesleyan University, as it is approached from the heart of Mitchell.

At the same time, there were storm clouds on Leland's personal horizon. The old trouble, which had sent him away for many months 10 years before, reappeared. In February he traveled to the helpful climate of Tucson for a time.

As part of Leland's regimen of work and rest, he developed his guidebook, which was rapidly becoming a reality. Joan was in Chicago, forwarding material to him. The secretary of the Black Hills & Badlands Association helped the printer put the book together. Their aim was to release it for the summer season.

Leland's attention to detail had characterized the revisions of *Editing the Day's News*, and this same effort went into his own Black Hills guidebook. If he loved anything more than journalism, it was the Black Hills. Back and forth went Leland's corrections, additions, and details of typefaces, make-up, and choice of paper and cover stock.

Leland assembled a collection of folks knowledgeable about the Black Hills to proof his work and make suggestions—his brother-in-law Cliff Wilson; Carl Sundstrom of *The Custer Chronicle*; Irma Wyler of Belle Fourche, who was Myrle Case's sister; the secretary of the South Dakota Historical Society, Col. Will Robinson; the general manager of the Homestake Mining Company—just a sampling of them.

That spring Macalester College invited Mr. Case to be one of a small group of alumni to be honored at an assembly marking the Diamond Jubilee celebration of the college's charter.

Leland replied, "As to whom or what I should represent at the convocation I know not, being a bit of a school hobo (by pressure of circumstances). I have attended what is now Black Hills Teachers College, Dakota Wesleyan University, University of Minnesota, University of Chicago, and Northwestern, as well as Macalester." Leland was invited to be the principal speaker. His 40-minute talk was a witty, scholarly low-keyed comment on the changes and the enduring values of his alma mater. Plainly, he loved to speak as well as to write.

By the end of June, 1949, Leland had to accept that his health problem was acute. He checked into Sanator, a sanatorium in Custer, in the heart of the Black Hills. He felt pressed to keep in touch with the progress of his guidebook, but cautioned the book's publishers not to tell anyone he was there. Only his sisters, his wife, and his brother Francis knew of his whereabouts, "quite literally in summer hibernation," he said.

Lee's Official GUIDEBOOK TO THE BLACK HILLS and the Badlands by Lee Case, official historian,came out in early July, 1949, just in time for the visitor season. It was a saddle-stitched paperback, 5 1/2 by 8 1/2 inches, with 112 pages, black and white photos, a good fold-out map, and detailed maps of specific attractions. The publisher was the Black Hills & Badlands Association. The book was copyrighted by Josephine Altman Case, which represented one of Leland's determined efforts to provide for his wife in case of his death.

Eventually the book ran to three editions, including a revision. It was the only book this bookman-supreme and editor-extraordinaire ever wrote and had published, excepting, of course, *Editing the Day's News* and *Around the Copy Desk,* which he coauthored. The little book was also full of stories.

110

This detail is from the description of U.S. Route 14 going north from Rapid City toward Sturgis:

"Dead Man Creek, 28.5 m., is a usually dry stream on the outskirts of Sturgis, so named because of what happened here to Charles Nolin.

"One evening in August, 1876, as bullwhackers were pulling yokes off sweating oxen at a camp, about a mile south of this spot, a young fellow loped in. The men knew him as Charley, who had been running a 'pony express' carrying mail at a dollar per letter from Nebraska into the Hills. He would 'take a mess' but he couldn't stop long, he said, for he was eager to make Crook City that night. This was to be his last trip. His mother had made him promise that, he confided, and he chuckled about it, even as the bullwhackers told him they had seen injun sign.

"Next morning they found Charley's body, mutilated and scalped. The Sioux had slashed his mail bags, tossed the precious letters to the winds, and had stolen his horse. The men scooped out a shallow grave and thereafter it became the custom for freighters as they passed to add another stone to honor a courageous boy. Now a monument marks the spot, flanked by black walnut trees grown from slips obtained at historic battlefields, Gettysburg, Antietam, Valley Forge, and others."

From his bed in Sanator, Leland sent copies of his book far and wide—over 100 of them. Letters came back from George Mickelson, South Dakota's governor; Will Robinson at the state Historical Society; the president of the Black Hills State Teachers' College at Spearfish; and dozens of others. Paul Friggens' letter meant much, because Paul knew writing and knew the Black Hills. Some of the letters contained criticisms or corrections, picking up on the minutiae of which the little book was full. The *Westerners Brandbook* in Chicago ran a review of the book, including the mention of a couple of historical points that needed correction.

This was the sort of comment Leland had hoped his book would elicit, to make the second edition more fascinating than the first and certainly more accurate. After all, he hadn't actually lived in the Hills for over 20 years and needed all the current local color he could get.

Letters poured out of Leland's room at the sanatorium. The director of Girard College in Philadelphia wrote to him asking if there was any material available on one of their former students of the last century named Cornelius Donahue. Now with time to read and dig, Leland wrote about Donahue, "not something that you will want to publicize widely, yet I would hazard the guess that few American colleges can boast of alumni who follow a Robinhood career and have so firmly woven themselves into Western American lore as has your Lame Johnny."

Leland cited the essentials of the story: Donahue died in 1920; age 46; occupation Road Agent; from a cultured Philadelphia family; a competent civil engineer and bookkeeper; accumulated a lot of cattle in Texas; when Comanches ran them off, turned desperado; held up the down-coach from Deadwood;captured by vigilantes who hung him on the spot. Leland also included a photo of himself leaning against the tree from which Lame Johnny was hung.

From his reading at Sanator, Leland picked up more useful leads that fed his thinking for the guidebook and his fascination with the Hills. His book mentioned the Thoen Stone, a slab of yellow sandstone that Louis Thoen had discovered on Lookout Mountain toward the end of the 1880s. The stone contained, scratched in it by knifepoint, a message from one Ezra Kind, sole survivor of a party of gold-seekers who had been ambushed by Indians in 1834. The stone bore all their names, and Kind wrote that he had lost his horse and his gun, run out of food, and was expecting the Indians would find him at any moment.

Leland learned that Charles Haas, an old-time rancher and avid naturalist, knew more about the story. Leland got in touch with Haas, recalling for him that when he was a young man working for the *Rapid City Journal*, he had done a story about a fire on Haas's ranch where the first professional motion picture to be shot in those parts was made. He understood that Haas knew the story about finding Ezra Kind's skeleton and his gun, and wanted Haas to share it with him.

Haas replied that local writers had no respect for his rights. "You want me to 'give' you a story it's taken me 25 years to track," he snorted, "and for which I have confirmative proof, after all I've put into it including several hundred dollars out of my pocket? Care to cover that expense? But about your guidebook, it's about the very best I've ever seen, and I bought a copy for each of my five sons, and I've made notes on 58 corrections or changes," the kind of stuff only a native would pick up. Leland traded him a fresh copy of the book for the one Haas had filled with helpful corrections. Leland also tracked down the great-granddaughter of one of the men whose names were on the Thoen stone, and asked her for any information the family had about his death.

Leland answered many of these letters by hand, in pencil, keeping a carbon copy. He proposed to Will Robinson that the state should erect some sort of monument to Jedediah Smith, near what was believed to be his trail, at Buffalo Gap. Robinson liked the idea, and thought a good bit about just where the monument should stand. Thirty or so years later, the Jedediah Smith Corral of the Westerners actually put such a marker in place, and Leland was there to help dedicate it.

In September Leland wrote, "We'll stay on here for awhile, but I'm industriously doing nothing but getting in a good rest which, I've decided, I really need." Joan was with him. Sisters Carol and Joyce took seriously the fact that the sanatorium food was not all that appealing. They would sneak in a good thick steak now and then to fatten him up. How faithful he was to the doctor's orders for rest was always a moot point. Leland used a stenographer a great deal during these months, but when Gordon Rollins dropped in from Dakota Wesleyan to see him one day, he found Leland lying in bed with ropes hanging from the ceiling and suspending a typewriter over his stomach.

Leland kept up the pressure on Bob Pennington, now executive secretary of Friends of the Middle Border. Bob's ideas of scholarships for Sioux Indian students were good, Leland told him. There was Frank Dorian, lineal descendant of the first white resident of the city of Pierre, but mostly a full-blooded Sioux, who was a natural-born artist doing some fine carving. He would benefit immensely from a semester in art at Dakota Wesleyan—you raise $50 and I'll match it. They did this, and today some of Dorian's excellent carvings, donated by his widow, grace the collection of the Dakota Art Gallery of the Middle Border museum.

The fund-raising efforts of Friends of the Middle Border had mixed success. The Chicago Friends chapter and the Chicago Alumni Association of Dakota Wesleyan University had taken to heart a goal of $10,000 in donations to come from their area. By dint of hard work and many hours the money was raised, but they were really troubled to hear that no such effort had been made in Mitchell, for Mitchell had raised very little money.

Ten years after the founding of Friends of the Middle Border, the question for Leland began to be how much FMB meant to Mitchell and what did it really mean in the long run for Dakota Wesleyan University. It had roused enthusiasm on the campus at a time of great need for inspiration. It had called forth a practical response among people who had things to contribute, both locally and in distant places like New York City. The concern was about who really cared about FMB and carried the responsibility? Leland had made his decision about his own career and was away in Chicago. FMB was dear to his heart, but he was not there. He could exhort, but he could not act.

Gordon Rollins, fascinated with FMB and what it could become, had developed great respect for Leland Case. Rollins's primary duty, of course, was to Dakota Wesleyan University, and the many problems facing a small church-sponsored college, so, in most cases, he could only advise the people at Friends. However, he wrote to Leland at Sanator, and journeyed many times in those months to visit with Leland in his sick-room.

Leland by nature was a very positive person. Only on extremely rare occasions did he put his disappointments about his brain-child into words, but he did unburden himself to Gordon. They swapped notes on conditions at Mitchell, what the short- comings were, and who was and who was not doing what ought to be done. They cautioned each other to burn these letters and notes. Gordon knew that not only were Leland Case and his brother Francis good for the University but

115

also that Friends of the Middle Border was too. He cultivated his touch with Leland for the sake of the University, but he did so out of genuine friendship. This was a convenient outlet for such frustrations as Leland occasionally felt since he believed that Friends of the Middle Border was an idea truly before its time. James Truslow Adams had seen it as an embodiment of his "American dream," the only cultural opportunity "in a vast area larger than all of France and pre-war Germany." Leland told Pennington and the people at Friends that 25 years from that time, some city in the Missouri Valley would be its cultural capitol, and if they were bold, that capitol would be Mitchell.

Over the next years Leland followed, with many proposals, and much money, and many disappointments, the progress of that prophesy. He had watched with dismay as the gift of Harvey Dunn's paintings went to Brookings instead of Mitchell. He watched as the concept of a center for western historical studies and anthropoligical, archaeological, and sociological research (implicit in the plan for FMB) was taken up with vigor and developed into the Center for Western Studies at Augustana College in Sioux Falls. Through it all, Leland maintained his positive approach to Friends of the Middle Border, and that will unfold in succeeding pages.

Early in 1950, Paul Teetor drove Leland from Sanator to Tucson, where the climate had proved to be so beneficial. Leland checked into St. Luke's In The Desert, sanatorium for men. He was most grateful. "I am nicely situated in a cheerful and attractive room down here," he wrote to Joyce and Cliff, "with a window looking out upon the gorgeous Catalina range. Food is good and everybody is friendly. Joan has found a little apartment not too far away—and she is delighted with it. So it looks as though the Cases are well set up for the rest of the winter!"

Joyce's affection for her little brother was always there. During a phone call shortly after Leland moved into St. Luke's, she started to ask him if he were homesick for fresh pink salmon, and suddenly became embarrassed when she realized her office was full of people.

The climate of Tucson and the rest it provided, were doing their work, since laboratory tests were coming up negative, showing great improvement in Leland's health.

CHAPTER VI
Home in the Desert Southwest

Leland's convalescence from this second bout with tuberculosis took longer than the first. It also provided an opportunity for a few men, who in the leadership of Rotary were not enthusiastic about his editorship, to move against him.

In March of 1950 the magazine committee had affirmed continuance of Leland's salary, and at the same time, had taken note of his long absence from the office. In June, the international board noted that Leland had been away from his desk for a full year. They moved to name him "consulting editor" at his present salary and to name Paul Teetor as editor-manager. Karl Krueger and Ainslee Roseen became assistant editors. Shortly afterward, Leland's title was changed to "field editor."

Leland took his new title seriously, and determined to spend something like half his time at it. He had a descriptive phrase for what he was doing with the magazine—"a daily grist of work."

At the time of his release from St. Lukes in the Desert, Leland and Joan bought property far out on the east side of Tucson, which was to be their home ever after. A lovely piece of desert with a gentle crown on which sat a small adobe house, it was Leland's "cactused acres," full of mesquite, creosote bush, palo verde, and especially the giant saguaro cacti. They referred to it as "Saguaro Homestead," and their "adobe abode." Next they acquired a Dalmation named "Fritz." On one of their first nights, just at bedtime, Fritz spotted a rattlesnake at the corner of their sleeping porch. "I tickled it with my .38," Leland said, "then finished it off with a hoe." After a couple of more episodes like this, Fritz was promoted from Watchdog to

Chief of Nasal Intelligence. In the following months, the Cases enlarged their holdings until they had over 100 acres.

The record of the next few months at *The Rotarian* is sketchy, but an "insider" has provided me with some insight into what happened. There were, my source tells me, two members of the board of directors of Rotary International who felt that Leland was arrogant and too independent of the board, so they decided to get rid of him. Accordingly, in the spring of 1952, the Rotary president decided that the field editorship was not sound corporate policy but was, rather, "social security" for the former editor, which he determined to end.

Leland was irate. He asked for and was granted a hearing by the magazine committee, which took place in June. All that the official record shows is, "At his own request, Field Editor Leland D. Case appeared before the committee to present a report on his activities since the creation of the position." Apparently this report included presenting the committee with a bill for overtime and extra work Leland had spent on the magazine over the past 22 years, amounting to many thousands of dollars.

After this meeting and further behind-the-scenes consideration, the magazine committee recommended that the function of field editor be eliminated and the work of the magazine be carried on by the staff in Rotary headquarters. The executive committee of Rotary International, acting for the board, took this action not by meeting but "by telephone and cable." They voted to pay Leland for editorial work that had already been agreed upon and to present him with a "gift" of $10,000. Effective September 30, 1952, he was retired from the employ of Rotary International with those pension rights to which he was entitled.

In the cool light of historical perspective, this seems a logical development. At the time, there were those who were undecided as to whether Leland had been treated fairly. With what little actual written record I have had to examine, one could make a case either way. I am tempted to say that although the action was inevitable, perhaps Rotary International should have exercised more gentility toward a man who had given them 22 years of outstanding professional service.

The magazine committee was quite pleased with Paul Teetor's work as editor. However, Paul, himself, was having health problems. In mid-July of 1952, Paul was replaced by Karl Krueger as editor of *The Rotarian*. Krueger was given full power to operate the magazine under the oversight of the board.

In the same action, the executive committee "considers the magazine division to be a part of the Secretariat and to function as a department of the central office." This was the end of the independence that Editor Case had established some 18 or 20 years before. Karl Krueger served as editor of *The Rotarian* from 1952 to 1974.

As the smoke cleared from all of this, Carl Miller, a member of the magazine committee from California and publisher of a group of local newspapers, wrote to the committee chairman, "Now that the Leland Case matter has been settled, and apparently in an amicable way, I hope we will all be fair in our dealings with Leland in the future. I strongly believe that his background of Rotary, *The Rotarian Magazine*, and magazine authoring is still of value to us, and I hope that none of us will frown upon Karl Krueger for seeking manuscripts from him. I believe Leland has accepted the committee's decision graciously and, for the good of Rotary, I believe we should all consider the past as bygones."

Paul Teetor was hired by Carl Miller as editorial director of Miller's seven newspapers. Paul and his wife Alta had four happy years in California, where Paul died in 1956. Miller, it might be noted, was the man who proposed that the *Wall Street Journal* bring out a West Coast edition, which they did.

Although Leland had found his departure from *The Rotarian* a difficult thing to accept, his sense of optimism seemed to carry him through it. To a very few close friends he confided his feeling that he had not been fairly dealt with. To most of his friends he spoke of too much overtime too long continued that had broken down his health. However, he said, an adequate staff had been built to carry the magazine forward, so it may work out for the best.

It had been a long and glorious chapter for the magazine, for the organization, and for Leland Case. To many it was the golden age of *The Rotarian*. Perhaps a less spectacular editor, more of a Rotarian than a journalist as Chesley Perry had suggested some years before, was in the best interests of the Rotary movement. At any rate, that is what transpired.

An evaluation of Leland's contribution as editor was written to him, at his request, by Edward L. Bernays of New York. Bernays was a widely-known public relations counselor to the government and to specialized publications, such as *The Rotarian* and a professor of public relations at New York University. He wrote:

"Every editor of a magazine like *The Rotarian*, which in a sense represents the organization both to its members and to the outside world, is doing a public relations job for the organization. By what he includes and what he excludes in his maga-

Leland and Joan Case attend a costume party at the Rotary Club of Tucson in 1951

zine, he is affecting the impression that both his internal public and his external public has of the organization.

"In the years 1930 to 1950 in which you were editor, there was a tremendous change in the public mind in its attitude toward Rotarians just as I would assume there was a comparable change in the attitudes of Rotarians themselves. It would seem to me from having followed your magazine in this period that it played an important part in changing the public symbol of the Rotarian from the H.L. Mencken-Sinclair Lewis-George Bernard Shaw cliche to one entirely different and much more in keeping with the reality, that is, that the

Rotarian is an interested, public-spirited and broad-minded citizen of the United States.

"It must be gratifying to you looking back on your years of editorship that you have played so important a part in the shaping of these new points of view."

In the next three years, the files at *The Rotarian* show that Leland was responsible, in whole or in part, for 39 items appearing in the magazine.

Living in the desert Southwest meant a lot to Leland. There was always something to see out his window, something not quite like the Black Hills, and certainly not like Chicago. In a letter to the Macmillan Company, with details of his work on revising *Editing the Day's News* Leland wrote, "STOP PRESS: just had an interesting diversion. Typing, I had an atavistic uneasiness, then awareness of movement out of the tail of my eye. Glancing up, I saw slowly slithering by in the sunshine, just outside my window, a rather long rattlesnake. So I stopped long enough to make it R.I.P. for him—and now proceed with the morning's routine." Shades of the boy at Bear Butte, with the porcupine he had killed with a rock!

A sad event had taken place in May of 1951. It was the death of Elmo Scott Watson, Leland's great friend and mentor, who had expended his life so fully and joyously for things he believed in. Leland wrote to his widow Julie, "Though I know that no words can bring solace at such a time, I can't forbear letting you know that I, too, feel a deep bereavement. Just twenty-five years ago, it is, that I first came to know Elmo and you. I have never forgotten how you two washed away that feeling of strangeness as I came in from the Black Hills and began to orient myself to university and to city life.

"There's a blessing in such memories—memories which, I know, are held by uncounted other folk. Through the years, warmed by your hospitality, I found Elmo and I had so many interests in common that I have long thought of him as a very special friend. It was a privilege, Julie, to have had that association. It was given to Elmo, as to few people, to enrich friendships with understanding and with comradship."

Leland might have been out of a job at age 52, but it certainly could not be said that he was unemployed. He worked on a revision of the Black Hills guidebook; he was revising *Editing the Day's News*; he was finishing two chapters for a book compiled by Roderick Peattie called *The Black Hills*, in which Elmo Scott Watson, Paul Friggens and others were contributing chapters. He was given the alumni award of merit by Northwestern University. He also followed up on leads in subjects that interested him, like the Thoen Stone, and he kept busy with things on his Tucson property. There were also Friends of the Middle Border, which was often on his mind, and The Westerners. It was still a full life.

Roderick Peattie was the editor of the American Mountain Series for Vanguard Press. When he approached the subject of the Black Hills, he found that the men he invited to write for him were eager not only to write about the geography, flora, and fauna of their beloved Hills, but to people their stories with human interest. And so they did. For he had chosen for his authors a coterie of friends—Badger Clark, Elmo Scott Watson, Paul Friggens, Clarence Paine, Ralph Hunkins and Leland Case. Watson, Friggens, Paine and Case have already appeared in this story. Hunkins was the superintendant of schools in Lead. Clark needs a bit more introduction.

Born in Iowa to the family of a Methodist pastor, Charles Badger Clark, like Leland Case, had come to the Black Hills when he was very young. His father had conducted the funeral for Calamity Jane in Deadwood when many thought the presence of her corpse would defile his church. Badger was about 17 years older than Leland. They met when Leland was in junior high school in Hot Springs. Leland was devoted to Clark throughout his life.

At age 21, Clark contracted tuberculosis. To recover, he spent four years on the Cross I Quarter Circle Ranch, north of Tombstone in Arizona, where he began to write poetry. He also lectured on poetry and life and faith, and was booked to speak all over the country. He built a fine cabin of four rooms with his own hands, "The Badger Hole" in Custer State Park north of Hot Springs, and lived there alone for 33 years. He was officially known as the Poet Laureate of South Dakota—or Poet Lariat, as Leland and the Westerners liked to say.

To write such a book for the American Mountain Series, Peattie wrote in his forward, you must look for "an enthusiast." His choice was Leland. Leland wrote two chapters in this most readable book. The first was called "Where B.C. Means Before Custer" and into these 45 pages he crowded a cavalcade of personalities who moved across these hills—people he had been studying ever since he was nine years old. In his second chapter, "History Catches Up," he brought General Custer onto the scene, and described the discovery of gold and how that changed the whole history of the area.

For one who wants to savor the romance, the beauty of the Black Hills, this book is a very good place to start. Badger Clark contributed three chapters. The first chapter in the book is his gracious, earthy description of the region. He wrote one chapter on touring the region and another on Mt. Rushmore. Watson's chapter is a very moving account of the Indian war-chief Crazy Horse, his fight for his people and for their way of life, and his death, in captivity, at the end of a bluecoat's bayonet. Friggins wrote a lively account of the cattle industry in the Hills region, from the first drive up the Texas Trail in 1871 to the early 1950s. Hunkins supplied two chapters, on the mineral resources of the Hills and on the great Homestake Mine, the most successful gold mine in America. Paine's chapter is a highly interesting resume of the lives of Wild Bill Hickok and Calamity Jane, weeding out the myth from the facts.

To a study of Leland Case, this American Series book is important. His two chapters are among the few things about the Black Hills, or anything else, that he wrote for publication in book form. For a man of his literary talents, this book, therefore, is a rare example. It brings together the man, blending his best writing skills with his lifetime love of this little corner of the world, and some of his closest friends who also shared this love with him. *The Black Hills* was published in 1952.

In the summer of 1953 Joan and Leland spent several weeks at Joycliff, his sister's cabin at Blue Bell near Hot Springs. They attended a Dakota Wesleyan alumni picnic at Rapid City, where Leland and his old friend Dr. Matthew Smith, now president of the college, had a good talk about Friends of the Middle Border. The thought had arisen that the man for DWU and FMB at this point was J. Leonard Jennewein, who was working at the United States Bureau of Reclamation in Huron. Jennewein was a mature and self-reliant professional whose presence would be felt all across the campus. A proposal was made to Jennewein by Dakota Wesleyan University.

Jennewein gave up his job at the bureau, where he had worked for 18 years, and signed a contract to teach half-time in English and in regional history, his great love. The other half of his time was to be spent developing Friends of the Middle Border through a three-year grant from the Board of Education of the Methodist Church, as a pilot experiment in regionalism in small colleges. Jennewein was a few years younger than Leland. Since he had a clear view of the obstacles preventing FMB from becoming what it really ought to be, and a firm conviction in the ideas that had brought FMB into being, he was willing to give it a mighty try.

"I will give full attention to your suggestions," he said to Leland. "You have the dream of FMB, surrounded by a practical concept." He saw the *Middle Border Bulletin* as a key to building the organization. The library should be built up to support a real regional study center. They needed regular programs for their members and for the community, on a monthly basis, and he had the first two all arranged.

It could be said, sadly, that in taking on Friends of the Middle Border, Leonard Jennewein signed his own death warrant. He had the intellectual, educational, historical, make-do-with-little organizational skills to cope with FMB, its problems, and its potential. As the years went by, he broke his heart on the rock of lukewarm financial commitment. Somehow, the money to make the dream what it should be didn't arrive, or came in insufficient amounts. What was needed to match his skills was a first-class promoter-fundraiser, or a fairy godmother. Jennewein tried, but that's getting ahead of our story.

For Leland and Joan, the stay at the Wilson's cabin that summer of 1953 was a happy time. They especially enjoyed the wildlife together. There was Minnie the Moocher, their favorite deer, with her sister Skinny Minnie. Cyril the Squirrel could be heard scampering across the roof, while Joe Blow, the buffalo, paid regular visits. They helped the Black Hills & Badlands Association entertain a group of travel editors, and recruited a number of good new outlets for the guidebook.

In Tucson, Leland and Joan did a good bit of work on Saguaro Homestead. They expanded the original dwelling with a lovely, ample living room, dining room, entry and porches; created a comfortable guest house out of a stable and tack room; and built a separate little building of sun-baked adobe for Leland to work in. Now, for the first time, he had room to spread out his things, room for files and for his library, and it felt good.

They also began to develop a section of their acreage for future sale, setting up a private water-cooperative and running in electric service. This became an important part of their future. Their land purchase had come at a fortunate point in their lives and in the life of the Tucson area, because the land was to appreciate greatly in value.

Leland accepted several more writing assignments, including one about the Black Hills for *National Geographic* magazine. He also signed a six-month contract as consultant to *Town Journal*, published in Washington, D.C.

At Friends of the Middle Border, Leonard Jennewein was coping mightily. He was a good teacher and worked hard at it. With the help of a bequest of $17,000, he had the long-hoped-for building constructed and suitably dedicated. Clinton Anderson, now a U.S. Senator from New Mexico, located the papers of Maurice Sullivan, the first biographer of Jedediah Smith. Senator Anderson purchased the collection and gave it to the

Friends. Although students were arriving to use the FMB collections in their studies, money was scarce, and was always a stumbling block.

Dr. Matthew Smith, in a swing through the East, visited James Earl Fraser in his studio, prodded by Leland's insistence that Fraser was committed to doing something for FMB. Smith returned from that visit convinced that Fraser, though friendly, had no intention of giving anything to FMB and, in fact, had destroyed a model that Leland thought had been promised to the museum.

Leland and Joan piled into their car and made a 7500-mile trip, Joan breaking off on her own at several points to do things she was interested in. They visited with Joyce in Hot Springs, whose husband Cliff had died. They visited Mankato and the senior Cases. Leland gave a speech at Sioux Falls. They had a good time at Mitchell with Jennewein. Joyce announced she would love to give some of Cliff's collection of Black Hillsiana to the museum, and Herbert Case would give a sermon cabinet that had been part of his ministry.

Perhaps the highlight of the trip for Leland was a visit to a ranch outside Denver. The Denver Posse, as their Westerner chapter was called, had invited all groups of The Westerners to gather for The First National Rendezvous, July 31, 1954, at Chief Colorow's Cave, on the property of L. Drew Bax, a rancher and student of Indian artifacts. One hundred and fifty men and women from New York to Los Angeles showed up. Arthur Woodward, flamboyant historian from Los Angeles, came dressed in his trapper's buckskins and fur hat and fired off his black powder muzzle-loader at appropriate moments. Leland's sister Carol and her husband came down for it.

Leland was thrilled! He had played a relatively small part in the Chicago group in the last few years, but he had done considerable "missionary work." There were now nine corrals, as they were mostly calling themselves, in order of their founding: Chicago, Denver, St. Louis, Los Angeles, New York, Tucson, Laramie, Rapid City, and The English Westerners Society, originally identified with the city of Liverpool.

Town Journal's editor, Carroll Streeter, was pleased that he'd gotten his money's worth from the consulting contract with Leland. In those six months Leland had sent him close to 50 communications outlining story ideas for the magazine, such as a background piece on Emperor Haile Selassie of Ethiopia, who was to visit the capitol, pointing out the emperor's warning to the world of what was to come before war actually broke out in 1939, and an article about the Mad Hatter theme for women's luncheons that was sweeping the nation.

As the *Town Journal* contract was winding down, a fresh assignment opened up for Leland. A news release from the Senate Committee on the District of Columbia, of which Francis Case was the chairman, announced that Leland D. Case had been appointed interim clerk to the committee for three months. The previous clerk had resigned unexpectedly, and Leland was to handle matters until a permanent one could be named. The announcement said his duties would include, "work with the Committee staff in preparing bills for introduction on opening day of the new Congress and study such matters as the integration in the schools, Potomac River pollution, and area traffic problems," not to mention some 25 or 30 bills that had been introduced at the request of District commissioners during the last session, but which had not reached final passage.

It was an exciting time for Leland to be in Washington, especially with this intimate connection to affairs on The Hill. Just coming to a head was the Senate investigation led by Senator McCarthy of Wisconsin to uncover Communist conspiracies in the United States. It became quite a witch hunt, and the air was thick with it.

Leland shared his Washington adventures with Joan, who remained in Tucson. He was meeting all sorts of old friends, such as Maurice Briggs from his days at Spearfish Normal School when he was 17 and Al Hagland, classmate at Macalester College, now assistant to the commissioner of patents. He also discussed the future with Joan. Tucson was a better climate, although "the action" was so palpable in Washington. He felt they both needed to get away from Tucson for at least a part of each year, not only because of the summer heat, but also because they needed mental and social stimulation.

Where did the Cases really want to base? Should they sell their Tucson property? What should he be planning—freelancing for which they could pick their own climate and that would be less confining or arduous than a full-time desk job? He was exploring possibilities and had already turned down two offers. Some folks in the National Parks Service were interested in him. Please put all this in our "thinking out loud" pigeon hole, he asked of Joan, consider it all, and let me have your ideas.

In February a tragedy of huge proportions hit Friends of the Middle Border. A fire broke out in College Hall at midday on a Saturday. Much of the choice material of FMB was still stored there and had not yet been moved to the new building. A great part of their best collections perished. Leonard Jennewein arrived at once, arguing with the firemen who refused to let him rush in to save priceless original documents and works of art. He wired Leland that night to report what had happened.

Dakota Wesleyan lost the entire building and with it their library. Fortunately for the college, business office records, registrar files, and student transcripts were stored in fireproof vaults and were saved. Harvey Dunn's *Dakota Woman* was also spared, since it was on display in Graham Hall, a women's dormitory on campus. Both Leland and Francis worked to make up this loss to the college and to FMB. They appealed to friends high and low for contributions to help in restoring both institutions.

Leland visited Mitchell to review the situation with Jennewein. Afterwards, Leland wrote to him, "Between chats with you I prowled over the debris that was once College Hall and books and priceless FMB items. And for a liberal slice of one hour I shared your—shall we call it a corulean funk? even wallowed in it. Why should I, ran my thoughts, ever again give an hour or an erg of energy to FMB? or a dollar?" Then, he told Jennewein, he thought of what had been accomplished by the efforts of so many, and the subtle but distinct change that the regional idea, represented by Friends of the Middle Border, had brought about on the campus.

This influence on the campus, this contribution from so many, placed a trust, an obligation and a responsibility on those who care, he wrote, that rested on Jennewein specifically. "They call for a new rebirth of self-reliance, nothing less than a revitalized effort to make, from what we can give, that which we want." Then he went on in five single-spaced pages to itemize things that should now be done.

If I had been the recipient of this list, a legion of sound points, I would have had two very distinct reactions. Leland's sense of reality and encouragement would have affected me the way grounding affects an electrical circuit; his suggestions were necessary, very helpful, challenging, even inspiring. However, the letter also would have driven me up the wall. Leonard Jennewein had already demonstrated that he could plan and move forward when his heart was in it. At this point, all he needed was to be helped to his feet; he had limited resources, but he knew how to use them. In Leland's days at *The Rotarian*, he had had a staff of 30 people; he had assistants, assistants to assistants, and troops of every description. Jennewein had no one, and he was teaching half-time.

Perhaps Leland should have been the man on the spot, but he was not. Leonard Jennewein was.

The fire at College Hall stirred a lot of action; funds were contributed to the college and to the Friends; Jennewein was able to liquidate past indebtedness and look ahead; people had a fresh impetus to contribute artifacts, papers, and memorabilia to FMB, so everything moved forward.

CHAPTER VII
Together Magazine

Lovick Pierce, president of the Methodist Publishing House, the publications and retail arm of the Methodist Church, sought Leland out in early 1955.

Three years before, the General Conference of the church had received a strongly worded communication from its bishops, calling for the rethinking of their publications program and for an instrument to reach more effectively into the homes of Methodist families. "Our people perish for the lack of knowledge, our causes limp because the news and the appeal never reach the man in the pew, our unity and morale suffer because ignorance of great issues and Christian duties lead to fear and suspicion and disunity.

"We call for a bold venture for the creation of a Methodist periodical, combining the best of modern craftsmanship and editorial skill and aimed at a circulation within twelve months of not fewer than one million copies."

At the time, *The Christian Advocate* was the main publication of the mid- century Methodist Church in America for reaching its clergy and its laity. It dated from 1826, a proud heritage of Methodist journalism. The bishops felt that something new was needed. Now Pierce contracted with Leland to bring him a formal proposal that would meet the modern needs both of the clergy and of lay families.

It was a stimulating challenge for Leland Case at a time when he needed it. He certainly understood the problem—similar to what he had faced with *The Rotarain*.

It was decided that two distinct publications would be needed. For the professionals, the concept was not that difficult. The other was the greater challenge—to produce something that the layman would want to read, be inspired by, find enjoyable as well, and that, month by month, would build the faith in them for everyday living in the modern world.

Then there was the challenge of church politics: there was a different point of view about how to meet this need for every shade of difference in the church itself—north, south; black, white; urban, suburban, rural; intellectual, workaday; evangelical, main line, liberal, conservative—and so on.

And Leland Case: An hereditary Methodist, who all his life had been drawn to the basic message of the Methodist Church—or, to be more exact, of John Wesley. Whose father had been given to the work of the Lord at birth by his mother, and who had toiled at the outposts of the church in America, living far from his wife and children for weeks at a time to accomplish his mission. Hymns around the Epworth piano by lamplight. Heroes—Jedediah Smith and Henry Weston Smith, Methodist pioneers. Editor of one of the most successful special-interest magazines in the world, which had reached its peak of prestige under his direction. One of the most purpose-oriented, results-oriented journalists of his day. At the height of his career.

As a journalistic professional, Leland applied himself to the need for improved service and an inspiring organ for the church cadres. They would call it *The New Christian Advocate*.

Leland's imagination, nevertheless, was truly galvanized to create something new for the man in the pew—or better still, for the man who hardly ever came to church. Leland studied the question in his quiet adobe office—where a quail might call outside the window, and the mesquite had leafed out from its winter sleep.

Leland's files contain reams of notes made as he developed his thinking on this project. I spent much time reading them, and I recount here my impressions of the process as he worked through it.

A cardinal rule that had been drummed into Leland over the years and that he in turn had drummed into others, was, "Remember—nobody is under any obligation to read what you print." A couple of generations ago the family spent long evenings together, reading—but no more. TV, radio, movies, the growth of sports, the car, the plethora of magazines available today—the competition for our leisure time is ferocious. We're thumbers, he knew; we read only what catches the eye.

It was the fringe membership of the church who needed the magazine the most, Leland thought. There was so much that a beautiful, well-produced magazine could give them—the excitement, the joy of living.

Leland had always felt the power of John Wesley's fundamentals. He liked to get down to Wesley's own base points, unadorned, uncluttered by interpretation. He went back often to the quotation "Is thy heart right, as my heart is with thine? I ask no further question. If it be, give me thy hand. For opinions, or terms, let us not destroy the work of God. Dost thou love and serve God? It is enough. I give thee the right hand of fellowship."

To succeed, he concluded, the magazine must not be complacent. It must catch and hold the eye of busy people. Pap would not do, nor guesswork sparked by cosmic brotherly love. The content must be on the cutting edge of modern thinking. It must bring a laugh, a sigh, perhaps a tear, and give something to think about, something to act upon, something to remember.

136

Leland studied the highly regarded *Presbyterian Life* magazine—bi-weekly, annual subscription rate $2.50, currently its circulation 855,000, one subscription for every 3.5 members. He did sheets of analysis—of the Methodist Church, its publics, and the varying interests of men and of women.

Of course, the job fascinated him. It involved not only thinking out the publication concept, but selling the concept to Lovick Pierce and his key men, and then that package had to be sold to the church. In the summer of 1955 he began lining up his material for the entire process—and also prospecting for the talent needed to turn the concept into reality.

Bart McDowell, whom Leland had recruited for *The Rotarian*, was one of a number of men whom Leland sounded out that summer. He was flattered that Leland thought of him for this new venture. But at the root of McDowell's thinking was his dislike of Leland's style of leadership. He was one of those who just did not want to work under Leland Case. He talked it over with Karl Krueger, his boss at *The Rotarian*, and decided not to accept. McDowell went on to a fine career at *National Geographic Magazine*, where he was one of their senior editors.

As the ideas began to coalesce for the new "peoples'" magazine, Leland searched for a name for it. "Although we may differ intellectually on many matters," Leland wrote, "we are brought TOGETHER in a love of God and of our neighbors. TOGETHER we create a family; TOGETHER we form a church; TOGETHER we build a nation; TOGETHER we bring peace on earth." He adopted the name *Together* tentatively early in 1955 and it stuck.

Leland made his presentation to the Methodist Board of Publication, in the fall of 1955, introduced to them by Lovick Pierce and his associates. They called it "the bold venture", after the bishops' challenge. He had prepared a dummy of *The New Christian Advocate*, designed to help the busy pastor, making it easy to see the contents of each issue, and with some new features, as well as several of the most effective old ones; and a dummy of the new magazine, *Together*. He identified leaders in the magazine field—at *Time*, *Life*, *The Rotarian*, *Nations Business*, *Arizona Highways* whom he had consulted, and Ben Hibbs, editor of *Saturday Evening Post* and himself a Methodist. Ben had summed up his convictions thus, "It has been conceived with spirit and imagination. Do what you have planned, and I believe it will go."

The plan for the *New Christian Advocate* and for *Together* was formally adopted by the General Conference at their session in late April of 1956, and the first edition of each magazine was to appear in October.

Warren Clark was chosen to be business manager of *Together*. He sent to all district superintendents of the Methodist Church an explanation of the new program: this is pioneering in the best Methodist tradition; to circulate not fewer than one million copies, every church will be urged to provide an annual subscription to every family on their rolls.

The headquarters of the Methodist Publishing House were in Nashville; editorial offices for *Together* and for *New Christian Advocate* were set up on Rush Street in downtown Chicago. From his original agreement to work as consultant for the creation of their new publications plan, Leland was asked to accept the posts of editorial director of general periodicals for the Methodist Publishing House, and editor of *Together*.

*Leland Case with (right) Lovick Pierce, President of the
Methodist Publishing House, going over inaugural copy of
TOGETHER Magazine, October 1956 (TOGETHER photo)*

This gave him editorial supervision over both magazines.
Editorial matters were to be entirely in Leland's hands; printing, promotion, circulation and advertising were handled by
Warren Clark and others in the Publishing House, and he had
little but advisory say in that whole side of it.

The two magazines appeared right on schedule in October
1956.

Together was designed to come out in the middle of each
month, to distinguish it from other magazines appearing in the
home. It was a beautiful magazine, employing the latest technology, as well as up-to-the-minute graphic style.

Then came the reactions. A lady in the office of the Black
Hills & Badlands Association, writing to Leland about their

handling of his guidebook, took the opportunity to tell him that *Together* was the most important and eagerly anticipated periodical coming into their home. There were legions of letters like this. And, immediately, there were strong criticisms from some members of the clergy. The Methodist Publishing House, having charted the course, stood behind Leland, and repeatedly thanked him for the thoughtful, comprehensive answers he wrote to critics, copies of which he sent to the publishers in Nashville.

Time Magazine for October 22,1956 made *Together* the subject of its lead story in their religion section. "The 1826 prospectus described the *Christian Advocate* as 'an entertaining, instructive and profitable family visitor.' This week, in one of the most ambitious ventures in the history of church publishing, the U.S. Methodist Church split the 130-year-old *Christian Advocate* into two visitors—one entertaining and one instructive.

"The instructive visitor is for ministers: a trim, digest-sized monthly...Initial circulation: 25,000.

"For lay families the Methodist Publishing House has launched a spanking new slick-paper magazine called *Together*. Edited by Leland D. Case, onetime editor of *The Rotarian* (circ. 302,202), this 88-page "Midmonth Magazine for Methodist Families" aims to have something for everybody. Manhattan's crowd-pulling Dr. Ralph W. Sockman contributes the lead article on "What My Religion Means To Me", but religion as such is subordinated to fiction and features; e.g., a movie guide with plus or minus recommendations broken down for adults, youth, children and family, a picture essay on a child with a cleft palate, an account of the world's record drop-kicked field goal (63 yards in 1915 by Dakota-Wesleyan's halfback Mark

Payne). Eye catcher is a color portfolio of portraits of Christ, vividly demonstrating how men have altered Christ's image to accord with the temper of their times and of themselves...

"Prepublication demand has been so great that the initial print order was upped from 600,000 to 700,000. By the end of the year, *Together* expects to have 1,000,000 subscriptions."

On the same date, *Newsweek* did a religion story on the new magazine as well.

Roland Wolseley, who as a young man had helped Leland put together his revision of *Around the Copy Desk,* was now teaching journalism at Syracuse University. He had been part of a small committee of professionals advising the Publishing House before Lovick Pierce had contacted Leland. He became a strong critic of the magazine.

He told Leland that he had recommended him to Pierce as a fine trouble-shooter but that he had never imagined they would place the magazines in Leland's hands. He felt that the magazine was not a real church publication, that it trivialized the church in features such as the All-Methodist football team carried in the December issue, and that the magazine did not take courageous stands on issues. There followed a vigorous exchange of letters, with copies to Lovick Pierce, the publisher.

Some of Wolseley's points, seen from the perspective of years, were sound criticisms, and in particular he demonstrated that Leland was making much of the praise of some critics while ignoring the opinions of others who were equally qualified to say what they thought.

From today's perspective it seems that some of the adverse criticisms ignored the original appeal of the bishops to create a new kind of magazine that would do something for lay families in the modern age, which was what the General Conference of the Church mandated the Methodist Publishing House to produce. Some of the critics really were not reconciled to the fact that two magazines with two different publics had taken the place of the old *Christian Advocate*.

The publishers received an estimated 6,000 letters, fewer than 10 of which asked their subscriptions to be cancelled, and about 50 of which were critical of an article, feature, picture, or perhaps, the format. All others were on the positive side.

As the months went by, the circulation built up through the efforts of the Methodist Publishing House and the bishops, superintendents and pastors as had been planned. By June of 1957 it had risen to 787,777. This was in contrast to the old *Christian Advocate, which* a year earlier had a circulation of 207,578.

There was real trouble in this side of the venture, however. The circulation department was just not organized to handle the volume. The mechanics of translating subscriptions into magazines mailed to subscribers were not able to keep up. Names were missed; people didn't get their magazines. Of course these were the days before computers. But *Together* was by no means the only magazine building a large subscription base. *Time, Newsweek, Life*—a great many magazines had mastered the absolutely essential techniques of mass circulation, and for much larger volumes than *Together* was dealing with.

The promotional side of the new venture also suffered. Time after time Leland proposed imaginative concepts to the promotion people for increasing circulation or for clarifying for their public the purpose of the magazine. Usually his ideas were either watered down or ignored. The quality he could build into the magazine was virtually unlimited, but what became of it once it was printed was severely limited.

In the course of working together, Leland Case and Lovick Pierce had become friends. Pierce knew he had the best in the business to head the editorial side of his new magazine. On that side he backed Leland one hundred percent. Leland, in Chicago, was given carte blanche to produce the magazine that the General Conference had called for. He was free to hire the people he wanted as his staff and to spend the money he thought he needed to make the magazine a success. So he did. As with *The Rotarian,* he built his staff with hard, demanding work with good pay, and with pride in their product. He often exceeded the established budget, but Pierce was basically pleased that a top-quality job was being done.

It was in the politics of the business-promotion-circulation side that *Together* suffered. For whatever reason, management never got from the business and circulation people the quality of performance that they got from the editorial side.

Leland felt that the church needed to draw strength, as well as direction and identity, from its heritage, and almost every issue of *Together* carried something that came out of this conviction. In the first 14 issues, for instance, there were eight articles and pictorials on John Wesley, six on his brother Charles, and one on their mother, Susanna. There were features on church architecture, church art and symbolism, and a series of stories on events in the life of the early church. The latter was illustrated by reproductions of fine paintings done for the magazine by Floyd Johnson, whom Leland hired as art editor, by Charles Hargens, and others.

One of *Together*'s art department staff in those first months of the magazine was Marilyn Sunderman. Marilyn was the only daughter of Esther, Leland's youngest sister, and her husband Ray. Marilyn was a fine young artist, whose initial artistic studies had been at Dakota Wesleyan University.

One of Leland's standing instructions to Floyd Johnson was that there be a dog in the picture. In an overview of the hundreds of illustrations Floyd created or directed for the magazine, a dog is included almost without exception.

The reader-participation features in *Together* drew tremendous response. Their first invitation to submit photographs on a theme for a pictorial—in this case "America the Beautiful"—drew 12,000 color transparencies. A call for crayon drawings by children received 1,800 entries. Regularly there were contests, such as for Family of the Year. Their story on "the all-Methodist football team" drew on the whole array of colleges and universities that had their roots in the Methodist church—ranging from the myriad of small places like Dakota Wesleyan University (where that first-issue story on the longest dropkick goal in football history had originated) to some of the nation's football powerhouses like the University of Southern California.

Leland had taken up life in Chicago again after six years of absence, and he and Joan rented an apartment on East Oak Street, near the office. Joan's heart had made the shift to Tucson to a large degree, however, and she was often there in the house she now loved.

Moving into his role as editorial director for Methodism's nation-wide periodical publishing entity, Leland applied himself to becoming conversant with the whole national Methodist scene—the current leadership, organizational structure, and the problems, issues and opportunities of the times. As he was

144

with Rotary International when heading up *The Rotarian*, he quickly became known widely in the church, as well as in the field of religious journalism.

In addition to his membership in the professional journalism society, Sigma Delta Chi, which he had joined before he worked for *The Rotarian*, he now took an active role in the Associated Church Press. Eventually, because of his service to the organization, he was named an honorary life member.

Leland's life was full. In the busy time of conceiving and developing the new magazines, he worked as well on the fourth edition of *Editing The Day's News* for the Macmillan Company. He had enlisted the help of Professor Floyd Baskette, who taught journalism at the University of Colorado. The book was published in June of 1956.

His assignment for *National Geographic Magazine* was to do a 7000-word article entitled "Back to the Historic Black Hills." What could be better recreation for him than that! During the summer of 1955 he and *National Geographic* staff photographer Bates Littlehales rambled around the Hills, starting at Sturgis and trekking up near to the summit of Bear Butte on burros supplied and guided by Sumner Bovee, one of the brothers he and Carol and Francis had played with all those years ago.

The result was an article lavishly illustrated with Littlehale's color photography and exuberant with Case's historical detail— his description of Calamity Jane's "vocabulary rich in ecclesiastical terms used in an unecclesiastical way", and the Methodist parson—Badger Clark's father—when told it was not a good idea to hold Calamity's funeral in a church responding, "She won't damage my church a bit. You bring her up the hill." Together they interviewed Iron Hail, one of the last survivors of the Sioux who fought at Little Bighorn. An interpreter was needed because he spoke little English. Within a few months of the interview, Iron Hail, thought to be 98 years old, was dead.

The article appeared in the *National Geographic* of October, 1956. He had a list of 126 people for the magazine to send copies to. Werner Janney, whose job at the magazine was to check the article for accuracy, wrote to Leland that, "in spite of the incredible amount of data that you crammed into your story—and the incredible amount of data that you therefore made me check—practically everything of any importance checked out to a tee, and whatever didn't were minor matters of description that somebody wanted to change. Thank you, Mr. Case, for being so accurate and so interesting."

In the midst of the excitement of the first issue of *Together*, and of the *National Geographic* article appearing, Leland's father, Herbert Llywellyn Case, died at his home in Mankato. The family gathered at the funeral, one of those rare times anymore when they all got together.

Somehow there was always time to keep up with happenings at Mitchell. Laura Gardin Fraser arranged to ship to Friends of the Middle Border her late husband's large plaster statues of Lewis and Clark—an incident that later stung Leland deeply when he learned that she had paid over $1300 out of her own pocket for the shipping costs.

Leland had in mind a Fraser Memorial at the museum, and Mrs. Fraser turned up a valuable cache of her husband's letters to a cousin in Belle Fourche, that was offered to FMB. At Dakota Wesleyan University there were faculty debates about some of the concepts Leland had outlined in his writings leading up to the founding of Friends of the Middle Border; Leland and Leonard Jennewein exchanged a number of letters about this, agreeing that regionalism in education remained a valid concept and that after 15 years the Middle Border idea was still worthwhile.

Leland suggested to Reginald Stuart, Director of the California History Foundation at Stockton, that they ought to develop an organization to honor Jedediah Strong Smith and to research and disseminate information about this staunch pioneer and Methodist. Stuart and his colleagues took up the thought, and the Jedediah Smith Society was formed.

Leland received a letter from Julia Watson, widow of his close friend Elmo, a letter both valiant and pathetic. She asked Leland to clarify for her the facts on the founding of the Chicago Westerners, and on Elmo's part in it. She had heard it stated at the Denver Corral that Leland was the generally acknowledged founder of The Westerners. If this was so, she said, she would renounce her honorary life membership in the Denver Corral that had been given her after Elmo's death, out of respect for his part in the founding, and she would also remove from Elmo's tombstone the bronze plaque given to Elmo by the Founders Society of America in recognition of his key role in its beginnings.

Leland replied in the warmest personal terms. He sent her copies of letters he had written recently to Ed Bemis, of the Littleton, Colorado, *Independent* and the originator of The Founders Society, who was trying to clarify the facts about The Westerners, and a letter he had written in 1949 with Elmo's concurrence to substantiate his contention that Elmo also should be recognized for his efforts to start the group. "Both statements", he added, "were done with regard to strict historical accuracy—and should settle the questions you have raised."

This whole matter brings up an interesting ambivalence in Leland's approach to the question of the founding. On the one hand, he was staunch in maintaining that Elmo share credit for the founding of Westerners. He did this almost invariably. For instance he insisted on it being stated on the letterhead of Westerners International all during his lifetime, and on the masthead of the *Buckskin Bulletin*, official quarterly publication of the organization. "A special purpose is to serve The Westerners, founded by Leland D. Case and Elmo Scott Watson in a Chicago suburb, February 25, 1944" reads the *Buckskin Bulletin* even today. In the 12 years that I worked actively with him, 1974-86, I never once heard him say anything, nor did I see anything written by him, that deviated from this.

On the other hand, Leland quite clearly acknowledged that the IDEA for Friends of the Middle Border, and its offspring, The Westerners, came from his own musings at Skansen in Stockholm in 1937, where he saw this striking example of building pride in a regional culture to buttress a people when they were in need of self-esteem, and of applying that to the need in depression-era Upper Missouri Valley country.

When someone like Ed Bemis pressed him for clarification on the founding, he would first of all cite the article in Volume I, Number 1 (April 1944) of The Westerners Brand Book of Chicago, edited by Elmo, which states "The idea of Westerners—informal get-togethers of men interested in Western history—originated during a conversation between Leland D. Case and Elmo Scott Watson in the fall of 1942. (Note by E.S.W.: "I feel certain that the first suggestion came from Leland, so he is entitled to the honor of 'Father of Westerners.'"

Marker at tombstone of Elmo Scott Watson in Evergreen cemetery, Lawndale Township, McLean County, Illinois (courtesy of Fred Egloff, Chicago Corral)

Then Leland would tell the story of Skansen; of thinking it over in Santa Fe in 1938 and discussing it with Clint Anderson, Hamlin Garland and others; initiating Friends of the Middle Border; then starting an FMB chapter in Chicago; and the Westerner idea flowering more vigorously than the chapter of FMB.

Perhaps you could explain Leland's position in two ways. The idea of Friends of the Middle Border was his; the extension into Chicago came about because the two men discussed it and went to work on it together. There was a passion for historical accuracy, and there was loyalty to a comrade-at-arms. Also, he had seen the same sort of question debated in the halls of Rotary, where Paul Harris clearly was the founder, but Chesley Perry put the energy into developing the organization.

At any rate, Julia Watson kept her honorary membership in the Denver Corral until she died, and the bronze plaque remains on Elmo's gravestone in central Illinois. The grave is in a little cemetery, "Evergreen," on property of Elmo's ancestor John Wiley Smith, one of the first settlers in 1834 in Lawndale township, Mclean County.

The Westerners in Chicago held a Founders' Night dinner in June of 1957. They rounded up expressions of appreciation from across the country saluting Leland as the founder; author Robert West Howard composed an official citation, and Sheriff John Jameson read it to the crowd at Ireland's Restaurant.

The citation pointed out that the word "Case" comes from the Latin *carere* and means "to take hold." It gave credit to Leland for starting and spreading the Westerner outfit—"It's a damned good thing", it said, "this meetin' is an anniversary celebration rather than a paternity suit. Think of all the Corrals, from Portland to Paris, that could get on the witness stand and testify 'Leland Case is my daddy.' "

Leland wrote to the four surviving members of the original group that had met to start the organization and shared the accolades with them.

In August, 1957, Leland Case circulated a memo to the editorial staff of *Together* and *New Christian Advocate*. "We've operated on a crash-basis," he said, "for a year, and now that we know what we are doing we will move on to a more orderly, planned operation. We'll begin to plan long-range to produce our magazines. So put down on your calendars right now our Quarterly Staff Planning Session."

Leland had reason to be proud of what they were producing in *Together* magazine. His friend Roy M. Fisher, Assistant City Editor of the *Chicago Daily Tribune*, had written him a thoughtful evaluation: "I have carefully gone through the first year's volume of *Together*, and want to say that the experience has been an inspiration to me. I have been inspired as a Christian, a Methodist and an editor." The main suggestion he offered was to keep it on its charted course. Don't fall for the temptation, he urged, now that you have gotten your audience, to veer toward a more church-centered content. It needs to remain primarily life-centered. You are covering strong subjects and covering them candidly and well.

Early in 1958, Leland had lunch with a small group of Chicago Westerners. They talked about a subject that several people in other parts of the country had raised: some sort of a hookup of corrals around the country and wherever else they were active, such as England. Philip Danielson was at the lunch. He was not one to let a good idea languish—or, in this case, even incubate. He put up $10,000 to create a Westerners Foundation, with another $10,000 pledged to continue it if the idea clicked. Danielson placed the money with the financial officer of the College of the Pacific, in Stockton, California, where he was a regent.

To some Westerners this was a great idea. To others, this was autocracy of the worst kind and it went against the democratic grain. In Denver, there was real resentment at the group in Chicago taking the subject so far without even canvassing the other units. The Sheriff of the Denver Posse, as that group was called, was inclined to be more low-keyed and amiable, or otherwise this might have been the end of any such idea. Hearing of the trouble, the Chicago group quickly acknowledged that they had definitely been in error, but that it came out of exuberance rather than arrogance.

A great deal of effort was required to heal this kind of damage, both in Denver and in other parts of the Westerners'

151

world—and reaction to a central coordinating body can still be felt among Westerners in various locations around the network.

Later that year Phil Danielson hired a young graduate student at the College of the Pacific, Glenn W. Price, to be the executive director of the Foundation, at a salary of $5000. One of Price's first duties was to file the incorporation papers for the organization with the State of California. On November 3, 1958, the Secretary of State officially chartered the Westerners Foundation. It was now a fact of life that there was a Westerners umbrella organization, with its office at the College, later to become University, of the Pacific, at Stockton.

To critics of *Together* magazine, Leland often quoted the admonition of John Wesley to "think and let think." Leland saw this as one of Methodism's chief strengths, that there was room for differences of opinion. He considered that Methodists were proud that their church was neither dogmatic nor authoritarian.

Throughout his editorship, some of Leland's good friends disagreed with him about his not taking a stand on controversial issues. The reason was very clear in his own mind. He saw the magazine as holding together people of varying viewpoints within its "family." He had seen the same thing with Clint Anderson at *The Rotarian* in 1932: let qualified people have their say in the pages of the magazine, on all important sides of an issue, and encourage the reader to think out his own position—"think and let think." Some Methodists agreed with this principle; others did not.

Although there was a good bit of heated controversy in some circles of the church about the value of the magazine, circulation in September, 1958, was at 935,045.

The division of labors at the Methodist Publishing House was, for a man attuned to the ways of commercial publishing as practiced around the country, a real trial. His colleagues in the magazine publishing field were accustomed to having their products live or die by efforts directly under their control. Promotion, circulation and advertising in the commercial world were under the supervision of the editor-in-chief. Here at *Together* he had no say whatsoever in how these functions were handled—or no say that mattered very much. How the magazine would have fared if he had had that sort of total control, we will never know.

Leland's mother, Mary Ellen Grannis Case, died in Mankato in August, 1959. All her children attended the funeral, and there were now a third and fourth generation to swell the gathering.

By its third anniversary *Together* was still hovering just under a million circulation. Of the 40,000 congregations in the Methodist church, there were about 8000 in the All-Family Plan for building circulation. But the quality of the product was impressive. Douglas D. Martin of the Department of Journalism at the University of Arizona wrote to him, "The book fairly stops you. My gosh, can you get enough material to keep up such an editorial pace? The thing is just astounding!"

The General Conference of the Methodist Church meeting at Denver in May, 1960, stated that *Together* magazine was now going into one out of every three Methodist homes in America. We have but started to tap the potential of *Together*'s special ministry to the local church, they said. The new goal set by the bishops was two million subscribers by 1964. "It can be done," they said, "and we are the people to do it!"

The Denver Posse of Westerners meeting in 1960 included (left to right) Robert L. Perkin, Fred Rosenstock, Dr. Arthur Campa (?), Raymond W. Settle who was the speaker, Leland Case, Fletcher Birney and Joe Koller of South Dakota.

Leland and Joan spent Christmas 1960, and several weeks that winter in Tucson. The change in climate was important for Leland. Apparently he never again had a problem with tuberculosis, and he took precautions to come to Tucson whenever he could from the rigors of the Chicago weather. Work on *Together* went on as usual, with constant dispatches back and forth from Chicago "by pony express."

As *Together* approached its fifth birthday, a decline in subscriptions was noticeable despite the call from the General Conference to increase to two million circulation.

Leland had built his relationship with Warren Clark, the business manager, as constructively and open-heartedly as he could. There were conferences every few months in Nashville or in Chicago. The product was there—Leland circulated statements from DeWitt Wallace of *Reader's Digest*, Hugh Curtis of *Better Homes*, Theodore Vosburgh of *National Geographic*,

154

Norman Cousins of *The Saturday Review,* and Ben Hibbs of *Saturday Evening Post.* And he quoted from the report by Starch, the publishing industry's most trusted reader survey organization, which said that *Together* has "an extraordinarily high readership."

In the area of reader participation, in May of 1961 alone the magazine had 1044 reader contributions exclusive of letters to the editor—501 manuscripts offered, 102 communications with their teen-age advisor, 47 nominations for Reader's Choice, etc.

But there were inner workings of the church and the publishing house. Behind the trumpet sound of the resolution passed by the General Conference to achieve a circulation of two million copies by 1964, there was a move to scale down the effort at *Together.* Leland knew—or perhaps sensed—this. He was quietly facing the fact that his job of getting the magazine into orbit was over and that its future now ought to pass on to other hands. He was gradually transferring the work of editorial director of general publications to Dr. Ewing T. Wayland, who had been editor of *The Christian Advocate,* and stepping into a consultative or advisory role.

Lovick Pierce had a major project at hand for his publishing house—to produce a history of that organization. He asked Leland to work on it with another of the staff, James P. Pilkington. Jimmy was director of personnel. He would work out of the headquarters in Nashville, and Leland would be set up in a new office in the Temple, the great old 27-story building on Washington Street in Chicago. *Together* and *The Christian Advocate* (the title *New* was dropped after its first few years) were moved from their location on Rush Street, downtown, to new quarters in Park Ridge, north of Chicago, where

THE MAN FROM THE HILLS

Leland at his desk as Editorial Director of Publications—TOGETHER and CHRISTIAN ADVOCATE, *with Dr. Otis Young, associate publisher of the United Methodist Publishing House, left, and Ira Allen, Methodist Missionary to Africa, around 1961 (*METHODIST PUBLISHING HOUSE *photo)*

they would share a building with some of the other Publishing House services.

As editor of a church-produced magazine for lay people, Leland had been in a unique position. He had not allowed himself to be fenced about by an ecclesiastical force-field. He was not a doctor of divinity or a cleric. He was a journalist; he was a man of the twentieth century; and he was a man of faith who believed in the Methodist Church. He would approach an Andre Gromyko or an Albert Einstein or a John Foster Dulles or an Erle Stanley Gardner for an article for *Together* as readily as he would ask a bishop of the church.

Did this make *Together* less suited to the layman, the man struggling to make a living, to raise a family and to keep faith

156

with God, or to know something about God? Or did it make the magazine more suited for him and his family?

Leland and Joan took time in the summer of 1961 to cross the Atlantic. Leland spent a week around England with Raymond Crist, managing director of The Witney Press of Oxford, retracing some of John Wesley's horseback ministry, poking into old burial places, feeding his spirit with the spirit of the founder of Methodism. He also took time to visit with members of The English Westerners Society, and with the Westerner compadres in Paris.

Leland's Aunt Edith Grannis had moved to Tucson with her longtime friend Mamie Martin. Back in the 1920s when her father had lived with them and Leland had stayed there while he taught at St. Cloud High School, she had prodded her father to write down his recollections of his life. Now she turned to these notes, and with Leland supplying the editorial expertise, Edith gathered together the many pages she had helped her father compile. In 1962 appeared *New Hampshire to Minnesota—Memoirs of Samuel Higbee Grannis (1839–1933)*.

The book was a document about America—the sturdy New England families that produced Samuel Grannis; the vigor of mind, body and spirit that took him to Minnesota; the honest business dealings that earned him respect; participation in the Civil War and all the heartache which that produced; the Sioux uprising in Minnesota in 1865; his courting of the finest young woman in his acquaintance; and the family they raised. To Leland it was what America was all about, and he said so in his foreword. It truly was something for succeeding generations to cherish.

Leland moved into his new set-up in the Temple building early in 1962. Although the new regime at *Together* was not made formal until November of 1963, it was taking shape rapidly, and Leland was now for all practical purposes a consultant to the editor.

He and Dr. Wayland had developed a good relationship over several years. Wayland was an ordained minister. They often talked in Leland's office, sometimes long rambling conversations about the church, the Christian faith and its teachings and how you lived them. Leland was known as a very private person, for all of his gregariousness. These times with Ewing Wayland may have been unique in Leland's life. Once the confidence was built they got into some of the problems and concerns of the politics that affected the magazines, and personal issues as well. On many a night Wayland would stay late at his desk to finish his work, making up for a long session with Leland that day.

Leland was informed that in early June of 1962 he would be cited Alumnus of the Year at Dakota Wesleyan University. Of course he had not graduated from Wesleyan, and had only put in two years there. But he had his honorary Doctorate from there because of his work on behalf of the college and of Friends of the Middle Border. Leland sent to a shop he knew in England for a ceramic bust of John Wesley, modelled from life in about 1790 by the renowned Enoch Wood. It had great value, and in appreciation of the college honoring him, he presented them with the 150-year-old bust. To Leland the bust dramatized the spiritual tie between Oxford University, where Wesley had studied and developed his principles, and Dakota Wesleyan.

Simpson College, of Indianola, Iowa, is one of the many

small colleges founded by Methodists. They invited Leland to address their Liberal Arts Festival, and he chose one of his favorite subjects—"Education: The Splendid Obsession of Methodism." They made him an Honorary Doctor of Letters. By this time Leland had also had an Honorary Doctor of Literature from Morningside College, in Sioux City, Iowa, where his father had had a church. Leland had memories from childhood of Morningside dignitaries at their dinner table because it also was a Methodist college.

Leland's brother Francis, in Washington, suffered a heart attack in March. Leland did not realize how serious his brother's situation was, and so it came as a shock when Francis died on June 22, 1962, at the Bethesda Naval Hospital. One of the comforting things for the family was that May Aaberg, as secretary to Francis, knew them all so well and was there to help.

Leland went quickly to Washington. There was a service on Sunday morning in the Metropolitan Memorial Methodist Church, with over 500 people in attendance. Then the family—Myrle and her daughter Jane; Lois, Joyce Case Wilson's daughter and her husband Phil Saunders; and Leland—with May Aaberg and several others of the staff, flew with Francis' casket to Rapid City in an Air Force plane. A service was held in the Methodist church, and burial followed in the Mountain View Cemetery, where Francis' infant son had been buried. Vice- President Lyndon Johnson led a delegation to the funeral, including Senate Majority Leader Mike Mansfield, Minority Leader Everett Dirksen, and 13 other senators.

Some years later the bodies of Francis and his son were re-interred in the Black Hills National Cemetery outside Sturgis, which Francis had helped to create. Meryl Case died in the spring of 1990 and is buried there as well.

159

Francis had made his mark on the political life of Washington and on the state of South Dakota. He had worked for honesty in government and in government contracts. He was known as a conciliatory force, but one who would stand firmly for what he believed to be right. He was a man of innate common sense.

The task ahead for Leland was to research the early beginnings of publishing in the Methodist church in America and the subsequent creation of the Methodist Publishing House. Now he needed a research assistant and secretary. He offered the job to Mrs. Ellen Blanchard, a young woman, mother of three small children, whose husband had recently died. Ellen had done some editorial work for the church, and she was bright, intelligent and capable. She was also a woman of faith. Friends in church circles said "What ever you do, don't go to work for Leland Case." But something about the job intrigued her. She prayed about it and accepted it.

"It was one of the most rewarding times of my entire life," she said years later. "It was the greatest growing experience ever. I thank God for it repeatedly. Dr. Case never expected more of me than he expected of himself. Instead of being a slave driver he was more of an encourager. I would say to him 'Dr. Case, I don't know how to do that.' He'd reply, 'Now's the time to learn.' He would not let me say no." Ellen Blanchard had not had a college education, but in the three years she worked for Leland she felt she had gotten far more than that.

It was a quiet suite of offices on the tenth floor of the Temple building, which they shared with another official of the Publishing House and his secretary. Leland had long had the habit of keeping a notepad and pencil by his bed and writing down thoughts that occurred to him during the night. Each morning he would come in with a sheaf of notes, and he and Ellen would have a conference.

Under his direction Ellen scoured the continent for material and references for their work. She was in touch with every library of any consequence that might have references for them. This included the Methodist seminaries around the country as well as the great special collections like the Bancroft at Berkeley, the Newberry in Chicago, and Harvard, Vanderbilt, Duke, the Library of Congress, and many of the public libraries.

As their research accumulated, Leland saw that they were compiling material that covered a wider field than that related to the background and early stages of the Methodist Publishing House. The Methodist Publishing House was, after all, only one among several publishing ventures among Methodists on this side of the Atlantic. They were developing a bibliography of materials printed by all the early Methodists in America.

The subject fascinated him, and he had Ellen compile everything they could uncover. John Wesley, for instance, in his several months in America in the 1730s, had put together a little collection of hymns. It was printed for him in Charles Town (Charleston), South Carolina, by Timothy Lewis, a man whom Benjamin Franklin had subsidized to start a print shop, an off-shoot of Franklin's shop in Philadelphia.

This was before John Wesley's transforming experience, which occurred after he returned to England. Wesley was still under the discipline of the Anglican hierarchy, and the booklet was not authorized by the church. Therefore the edition was burned, and apparently only two or three copies exist. It was dated 1737.

Leland began to build his files on "eighteenth century American Methodist imprints", as he described them, and became quite well known for his studies on the subject.

Leland and Joan kept up their relationship with Laura Gardin Fraser after the death of her husband. During a visit to her home and studio in Westport they saw three tremendous panels that she was doing, to be cast in bronze. Their subject was the history of the United States. The work had been commissioned for the entrance to the library being built at the U.S. Military Academy at West Point.

Leland studied her exquisite clay models, with their high-relief portraits of people and events. He asked her why Jedediah Strong Smith was not included. "I don't know about Jedediah Smith", she replied. With her permission Leland described his hero and his role in the opening of the West. But, she said, the work was too far advanced to permit adding this unknown man. Leland sent material on Smith to her over the next months, with a hope that something might work out.

At the end of the year, Mrs. Fraser told Leland that she had consulted the committee responsible for the historical aspect of the three West Point panels, and had shown them how she could rearrange Davey Crockett and Johnny Appleseed to everyone's satisfaction, and Jedediah Smith was now in the panels. In fact, when the bronzes were poured, she arranged to have a copy of the detail of Jedediah Smith cast for Leland.

The other thing Leland and Joan had noticed in the studio of Laura Fraser was a plaster frieze she had created of the Oklahoma land rush. A magnificent thing, 20 feet long, it was full of figures frozen in action. Leland's friend Dean Krakel, of Colorado and Wyoming, was Director of the Thomas Gilcrease Institute for American History and Art in Tulsa, Oklahoma.

162

Leland wrote to Dean and urged him to see this important work—it ought to be in a place of honor in Oklahoma, Leland told him.

Krakel and his assistant, Paul Rossi, called upon Mrs. Fraser in her studio in Connecticut. They were captivated by the artist herself, by the Oklahoma frieze, and by the wealth of art work both of her own and of her late husband's, that she had massed around her in the studio.

Alas, the Gilcrease Institute had no money to do anything about it. But the seed had been sewn in the fertile Krakel mind.

Shortly after this, Krakel was hired away by the brand-new National Cowboy Hall of Fame & Western Heritage Center in Oklahoma City; Rossi took his place at the Gilcrease. In the ensuing 10 years, Dean Krakel made good use of the introduction to Laura Fraser that Leland had instigated.

Both Krakel and Rossi were involved in The Westerners. Krakel had helped to found the Laramie, Wyoming, corral in 1953, and was associated with Leland as long as Leland lived. Rossi loves to tell how Leland would inspire him to develop new corrals. Rossi travelled a good bit as Director of the Gilcrease Institute. Leland seemed to know of his travels and would phone him and urge him to see someone Leland knew and get a new corral going in whatever city he was visiting. Paul did help to start a corral in Tulsa, and he and his wife Florence had a hand in organizing a second one in Tucson, the Santa Catalina Corral (there are now three in Tucson).

Lunchtime saunterings through bookstores gave rise early in the 1960s to Leland's informal association with three men who shared one thing in common with him—the love of the Black Hills. There was Melville C. Williams, Chicago attorney who had grown up in Rapid City with a great love of the Hills;

163

Dean Esling, also an attorney, had been brought up in Deadwood and had been County Attorney there. Occasionally there was a member of the Chicago Symphony Orchestra whose name has been lost to us. Leland called the group The Chicago Tipi Ring, and mostly their meetings came about because Leland got the urge to talk Black Hills and would telephone to see who was free for lunch.

Williams had met Leland in the early 1940s, but had not really gotten to know him until he joined the Chicago Corral of Westerners in 1959. Leland attended the Westerner meetings only once in a while, and Mel had the feeling that it was because Don Russell, the spark plug of much that happened in the group, was edgy about Leland getting so much credit for its founding.

Mel enjoyed the Tipi Ring. One lunchtime he and Leland were the only ones able to come. Leland began reminiscing about his days in Paris, and he confided a story about his poor knowledge of the French language that had been a very great embarrassment to him at the time. At a dinner party in a private home, he wanted to compliment his hostess on the excellent fish that had been served. As he leaned toward her what he said stopped the conversation of the entire company. Instead of the word "poisson" for fish, he used the word "poitrine", and what he said in fact was, "Your breast is magnificent." We are left in the dark as to the outcome of this incident!

Early in 1963 Leland made a trip out to San Francisco and Los Angeles, researching the publishing house history. He included a stop at Stockton, and there met Dr. R. Coke Wood of the department of history of Stockton Junior College. Dr. Wood was vitally involved in the several organizations of California historians and was a member of the Jedediah Smith Society, as well as The Westerners. They became fast friends.

Leland was beginning to think about the eventual disposition of his library, particularly his collection of books and materials about the West. His first thought was Friends of the Middle Border. The concept of a research facility there was part of his original dream. Francis Case's papers were there. Leonard Jennewein's library was going to Dakota Wesleyan. He calculated the value of his books and an endowment he would leave for upkeep of them to be about $25,000. He opened the subject with Jennewein, and with the University president. But he couldn't elicit the interest he felt ought to be forthcoming, from President Early or the university.

Leonard Jennewein was ill, and his wife was in poor health. But he had produced *Black Hills Booktrails*, a bibliography of materials on the Black Hills, and he had asked Leland to write a foreword for it. It was a nicely produced book and sold well among collectors.

CAPTER VIII
No Such Thing as Retired

In April 1963 Leland made another trip to England. He was digging up more material for the history of the publishing house, but his lively mind was also developing other things. The Methodist Church in England was having a hard time financially, and Leland sought to help. He proposed that Methodists in America might pick up the tradition of John Wesley's *Methodist* magazine. Wesley had begun it in 1778 as *The Arminian Magazine*, preserving in that name his link to the theologian Jacob Arminius whose work had meant a great deal to him, but a few years later he had revised the name. The English were planning to discontinue publication, and Leland felt there must be a way for the Methodists in America to perpetuate this valuable link with their beginnings.

This historical continuity was the type of concept that made tremendous sense to Leland, but which did not necessarily excite others to the same degree. The thought of somehow perpetuating the tradition of John Wesley's *Methodist* magazine was a concern for which Leland worked for the rest of his life.

The oldest Methodist church building in continuous service anywhere in the world is Saint George's, in downtown Philadelphia. Its pastor, Dr. Frederick E. Maser, had created the Saint George's Award for distinguished service to the Methodist Church in the United States. It also served to keep the old church in the limelight nationally, for it is a shrine as well as a parish, and a small parish at that. The award consisted of a gold medal suspended from a scarlet ribbon. In October, 1963, Leland D. Case was one of four men honored with this medal. Dr. Case was cited for his wide travel in the interests of the

The St. George's Medal for distinguished service to the Methodist denomination, presented in 1963 by Bishop Fred P. Corson (left to right) to H. Conwell Snoke, Bishop T. Otto Nall, Frank E. Baker and Leland Case

church and honored with these words: "He has labored tirelessly, with ability and imagination, to raise religious journalism to a new and higher level. He has used the resources of *Together* magazine in particular to set forth the history of Methodism, making Methodists everywhere proud of their heritage."

The four awards were presented by Bishop Fred Pierce Corson, president of the World Methodist Council, at a formal banquet at the Warwick Hotel. It was a gracious occasion for Joan and Leland. It also cemented a friendship between the Cases and Dr. and Mrs. Maser.

The invitation for December 20, 1963, read, "You are cordially invited to attend an appreciation dinner honoring Dr.

Leland D. Case, former Editorial Director of *Together/Christian Advocate* Magazines to be held at 7:00 o'clock, in the Town Room of the Knickerbocker Hotel. R.S.V.P Ewing T. Wayland."

It was 10 below zero outside, but a hundred people gathered to say "thanks" to Leland. Professional colleagues, Publishing House people—and thirteen of his family—Joan; all three sisters, Joyce and Carol down from Hot Springs and Esther from LeSueur, Minnesota; Francis's widow Myrle with her daughter Jane and granddaughter Catherine from Washington; Aunts Edith and Mamie from Tucson; Marilyn Sunderman from Honolulu; and a slew of cousins from Iowa, California, Wisconsin and New Mexico.

A memento was put together for Leland, a book of remembrances. It was nicely bound, was three inches thick, and had gold embossing. It contained letters from Leland's family and messages from 354 others, mainly Methodists, ranging from the cabinet of the United States and Congress, to governors of Arizona and South Dakota, presidents of colleges and universities, journalists, clergy, businessmen, Rotarians, authors and artists, and old friends. To browse through this book was to journey through 60 years. For those who had worked with, or against, Leland in the Methodist Publishing House, it was a chance to say, "You did a great job and I'm sorry I created so many problems for you." A sampling of the letters include:

"How we wish Francis were here to write this note of appreciation to his kid brother, the lad whose mind was always bubbling over with ideas. You are not a dreamer but a man of action, seeing ahead the values in the history and mementos of the Middle Border with a burning desire to put all in their proper place." -Myrle Case, Jane and Catherine Commander.

168

"Recalling claim days, when we followed rabbit trails to the traps, your fertile imagination baited my every step! My pride and admiration in your ability and accomplishments are matched only by your own earnest devotion and sincere dedication to *Together* and *Christian Advocate*."—Carol Case Goddard.

"You have given the Methodist Church the best years of your life. All of us are indebted to you for the new vision of journalism within the boundaries of the church which has brought new and rich points of view of lasting value. You have exercised an influence which is seldom enjoyed within the life experience of any person."—Harold M. Dudley, Public Relations, The Washington Liaison Service, Washington, DC.

"The concept of *Together* when the venture was started in 1956—I was against everything about it. Now eight years later I want to write this letter to say that I have changed my attitude. I take off my hat to you. For you have done something of the impossible, and we stand in your debt."—Harold Ehrensperger, Boston University School of Fine and Applied Arts.

The grass-roots journalists around the country, from the heartland of the church to small publications and large, added their voices. Some of them Leland had met at regional conferences or through correspondence, but many he had not.

"We have had the best of the best among us."—William D. Leavitt, Director, Methodist Information, Little Rock, Arkansas.

"Somehow you were able to see this Methodist Church as ten million individuals and not just a mass of millions. All of the material in *Together* seemed to have some of those individuals in mind."—Harold L. Hermann, General Board of Evangelism, The Methodist Church, Nashville, Tennessee.

Many of these people, in their own words, said the equivalent of, "My own personal relationship with you has been one of the rich experiences of my life." Many of them were people I had not come across before while reviewing the volumes of Leland's correspondence.

There are many letters from former staffers who went on into other publications and whose careers felt the influence of Leland's training and guidance. There was a black staffer who thanked Leland for helping him along the way.

Nine years after these words of praise and thanks were given, *Together* disappeared from sight. Its circulation had dipped below 250,000. The church did another extensive review of publication needs and created, for the layman, *United Methodists Today*, a digest-sized monthly. The clergy's *Christian Advocate*, a title that went back to 1826, was discontinued and replaced with a special edition of a new magazine called *Today's Ministry*.

Leland's profession was the printed word or, more properly, the printed page. There were other significant accomplishments in his career, but *Together* represented the best he had to give during more than 30 years in the field of journalism.

Like me, Leland Case was a PK, a preacher's kid (I have four generations of clergy behind me). He also chose to serve as his talents directed him which did not include holy orders.

Together magazine was his way of sharing the faith with the lay person. He put everything he had into it. The kid from the Black Hills had done his best on a big stage, where all the world could see.

Dr. Robert Burns, president of the Methodist-oriented University of the Pacific at Stockton, California, suggested to Leland that, when he was ready to move from the Methodist Publishing House, he might come to Stockton. There was a strong sense in Dr. Burns and his colleagues that the university should develop an important program of historical studies. The California History Foundation was located there, based to a considerable degree on the special library collection of Reginald Stuart, whom Leland had inspired to found the Jedediah Smith Society. President Burns also had an interest in establishing a comprehensive collection of Methodist materials for a west coast Methodist center at the university.

Leland thought about this invitation a great deal. He mulled it over with friends, in particular with Ray Billington.

The name of Ray Allen Billington belongs in any account of the life of Leland Case. He was teaching history at Northwestern University when The Westerners was founded and became an early member of the Chicago corral. Over the years Dr. Billington became one of America's most distinguished historians. His career took him to the Huntington Library in San Marino, a suburb of Los Angeles, where he joined the Los Angeles corral. Ray strongly believed in The Westerners, in their value to the cause of American history. As an academic, he believed particularly in the informality that they imparted to this often stuffy subject. He was a staunch supporter of the effort to build a coordinating umbrella for the loose collection of corrals. On research trips for the history of the Methodist Publishing House, Leland had consulted not only with Ray about the prospect at the University of the Pacific, but also with Coke Wood. He became more familiar with the whole world of historical studies in California.

Back in the office at the Temple, Ellen Blanchard steadily compiled the files of historical material concerning the Publishing House. She also handled plenty of correspondence for Leland's other interests, which was usually dictated on a Stenorette machine and transcribed by the secretaries out at Park Ridge.

It has interested me to note that Ellen Blanchard and practically everyone else who typed Leland's letters during his professional career were crackerjack typists. The typographical errors detected in the hundreds and thousands of pages of letters, reports, proposals, articles, and memoranda that I have surveyed over two years of research might be counted on 10 fingers, or less. This would probably indicate not only that the boss was demanding and sent typos back for rework, (for we are talking about the age of carbon paper, not photocopiers or word processors) but that it also represents the calibre of people Leland was willing to work with and also the calibre of people who were willing to work with Leland Case!

My wife and I visited with Ellen Blanchard in the summer of 1989. She told us that after she had become accustomed to working with Dr. Case (she always called him Dr. Case even in 1989), he handed her a couple of items one day and said, "You draft these replies." She said, "What? I can't write your letters! You are renowned for your letters!" He said, "You know how I think and how I phrase things. You write them and I'll sign

172

them." She was flabbergasted. But he meant it. She tried, and before long, she routinely drafted letters in styles she knew he would use when working with specific individuals and in specific situations.

In his professional life, Leland had a capable and adequate staff around him. Often others with whom he was dealing either did not or had more limited staff assistance. For instance, Leonard Jennewein must have found it irritating and frustrating for Leland to pour out pages of things for him to consider and to act upon. He might well have been able to cope with them and return measure for measure, but he worked alone and he rarely had anyone to do a letter for him, much less a report or research.

After Leland retired, his correspondence would sometimes be delayed for days waiting to be transcribed. Nevertheless, until he died, he usually had someone doing his letters for him. On the other hand, he always had a typewriter by his desk, whether in *The Rotarian* or *Together* offices, at the Temple, or back in his adobe office in Tucson. Some things he drafted by hand, and others he drafted, quite handily—expertly in fact, by typewriter, like the jouneyman journalist that he was. He had an old standard L.C. Smith machine—Elsie Smith, he liked to call her.

To say that Leonard Jennewein carried Friends of the Middle Border on his back would be almost literally true. In early 1964 he concentrated regularly three to four hours a day on it, training and helping the student attendant who was working there, developing a student program, arranging for and working himself on physical needs, such as the heating plant. In addition, he had his regular teaching load at Dakota Wesleyan. He declined an offer to return to government service at twice the salary

173

DWU was paying him. He spent three weeks cleaning out the basement to get it ready for exhibitions. He and Gordon Rollins laid tile for the basement floor during vacation.

Jennewein and Case clashed frequently on their concepts for the library. Leland had vividly in mind the fire in 1955 that had wiped out so many of their precious things, and he sought to compensate by having duplicate record- keeping. Jennewein wanted the library system to be compatible with the system at Dakota Wesleyan and saw no reason to deviate from standard library practices. They almost parted company on this issue. It went back and forth for months, as if neither understood they were trying to equate apples and oranges.

Leland eventually withdrew his suggestion of combining his and Jennewein's libraries. He would find a place for his books where they would be appreciated, he said, in something of a huff. He did, however, relegate most of his Middle Border materials—those that were not duplicates of Jennewein's—to FMB.

And he instituted a move to obtain an honorary doctorate for Jennewein. It took time, but finally an honorary Doctorate of Literature was awarded to Leonard Jennewein—posthumously, in 1968, by Illinois Wesleyan College.

Despite their differences, each appreciated the other. "You just about drive me crazy sometimes," Jennewein said to Leland. "But surely only small minds will try and downgrade the importance of FMB or of your contribution just because, so far, we haven't been able to put together a machine at this end that can measure up to the idea or keep up with you."

Jennewein worked hard to build up interest among the board of directors to plan and to raise funds, always the weakest side of the institution. He was convinced that Friends of the Middle

Border was the element that made Dakota Wesleyan a different and a better school than the other schools around it. He felt that the cultural center which FMB represented and its regional research capability were sound elements that needed to be developed. "If we don't do it", he kept saying, "someone else will."

Leland was well-known in Methodist circles for his interest in history. Bishop T. Otto Nall, an officer of the Association of Methodist Historical Societies, had undertaken for the Association the creation of a new committee on shrines and landmarks for the church. He chose three men to put this work together. One of them was Dr. Leland Case.

The shrines and landmarks work appealed to Leland, and over the next few years it became quite a commitment for him. A procedure was set up for the consideration and acceptance of any particular site or building as an official shrine of American Methodism. Leland looked to a number of the historical societies of the land as models, in particular those of Massachussetts and California and his friends at the National Park Service. He took great pains to design markers for historic sites and for the graves of Methodist clergy that incorporated the symbol of a preacher on horseback.

As Leland moved into this area of the Methodist world—historical preservation and promotion—he found himself championing a particular cause time after time and year after year. The cause, which might seem obvious to some, was: Why not include and make use of the laymen who have expertise in the particular field of interest—in this case, history and historical preservation. The issue, boiled down, was—church commissions and boards (and therefore the power) are dominated by and in many cases totally composed of clergy; why not let the laymen in!

Strange as this may seem, it was a battle. Leland, himself a layman, had broken some new ground, along with Lovick Pierce, in becoming editorial director of general publications for the church and editor of *Together*. He did not even have an earned doctorate—and the Methodist Church establishment loved doctorates. During his time on what became officially the Shrines and Landmarks Committee, he used, and promoted the use of, professional historians and preservationists in the committee's work.

Another cause that Leland espoused concerned the Association of Methodist Historical Societies. The Association produced some valuable materials; yet the materials were mostly available only to their own members—and their membership was composed only of Methodist historical societies. Leland proposed to Dr. Nall that they offer memberships to individuals. Dr. Albea Godbold, Executive Secretary of the Association of Methodist Historical Societies, was one who liked the idea and urged Leland to propose it to the General Conference.

"And by the way", Godbold wrote to him, "I am not familiar with the word 'bevisioned.' It is not in my *Webster's New Unabridged Dictionary.*" Godbold, who was new to Leland Case, had run into Leland's creative use of the English language.

We have a word-picture of Leland at work on these Methodist projects in the first years of his retirement. It comes from the Reverend Ernest Case, of Boston (no relation to Leland but always referred to fondly by him because of their common name). They served together on the General Commission on

Archives and History. Ernest Case wrote to me: "My memory of him is that of his commanding presence at a meeting. Tall and dignified with white hair and well- groomed moustache, Leland would boldly stand to speak on an issue. As he became excited, if there were opposition to his idea, his cheeks became a high pink in color, in marked contrast to the white of hair and moustache. Becoming more animated his cheeks became rosier. He held to his point with stubborn tenacity, but always with grace. Leland always accented the positive contributions of an individual; he tried to make every person feel important."

Leland visited with the Ernest Case family for a few days in their home in Boston. His host, realizing how keen Leland was on picking up good used books, drove him to several second-hand bookstores in the greater Boston area. Leland bought a great quantity of books, and they stacked them in the hall of Ernest Case's parsonage. When it came time for Leland to leave, he asked his host if he would pack them and mail them to him in Tucson. Leland either had no idea of the size of this task, or he assumed that Ernest Case would be delighted to help. At any rate, the amount of work that went into meeting this simple request is what lingers in the mind of Ernest Case!

On a June evening in 1964 Leland fulfilled an engagement to read a paper at the Mississippi Valley regional meeting of the Bibliographic Society of America, in St. Louis. He had been invited by the director of libraries of the University of Kentucky. This was to be a scholarly paper entitled "Origins of Methodist Publishing In America," on Leland's research into 18th century Methodist American publications. He sought advice about the propriety of including a little human interest in his paper for this erudite audience. It would be hard to imagine

Leland giving a paper that did not contain human interest, but he wanted to be sure he wasn't out of order.

The Bibliographic Society published his talk in their *Papers of the Bibliographic Society of America*. This was one of those high points in Leland's life, perhaps the only time something of his was published in a scholarly journal. He drew up a list of 131 people to be sent reprints—the whole spectrum of his friends: his family, Methodists, historians and Westerners, educators, Friends of the Middle Border colleagues, his journalist friends over the years, librarians, South Dakotans.

By mid-summer of 1964 Leland had decided to accept Dr. Burns's offer at the University of the Pacific. He would begin his work there in the fall of 1965. And having decided, he moved steadily toward it in his thinking.

In accepting a post on a college campus for the first time in 40 years, he was conscious that his only doctorates were honorary ones. The publication of his work in the Bibliographic Society journal was the sort of prestige he knew would set well with his academic colleagues-to-be.

It has surprised me, in studying this period of the Cases' life, to find that Leland was giving serious thought to selling their Tucson home and moving permanently to California. He floated several feelers toward people who might like to purchase their property.

I suppose that having lived in the Black Hills, in Chicago for nearly 30 years, in Washington and San Francisco briefly, he could well imagine another move to a metropolitan area or to a vibrant growing region like central California. At any rate, the Cases gave the matter a good deal of thought.

Albea Godbold asked Leland to head a committee to create a filmstrip celebrating the 200th year of Methodism in the United States. The celebration was for 1966, and great preparations were being made throughout the church. Leland attended a meeting in Nashville to get the filmstrip project launched. The Television, Radio & Film Commission of the church (TRAFCO) was to produce the product. The budget for the project was set up by the historical commission for $4000, of which they had allocated $500 for a writer's fee. Leland offered to do the writing as a contribution. TRAFCO's people took pains to define for him the differences between writing for print media and writing for audio-visual purposes.

Leland did a draft of the filmstrip, with the title "Live or Die, I Must Ride". The TRAFCO people had some suggestions, which he did not take too seriously—about the length and the amount of factual material appropriate to a filmstrip. It is interesting that Leland, the consummate professional journalist, did not feel the audio-visual experts had anything to teach him about their medium.

He invited Lowell Thomas to record the narration, and to do it without charge as a contribution to the Methodist Church. Leland always knew which of his colleagues were Methodist and might be approached for such things. The film strip narration was recorded by Thomas, and more than 400 copies were distributed during the celebration year.

Leland and Joan had Christmas, 1964, at home in Tucson, and Leland was there for six weeks or so. The thought of moving permanently to California was strong, and they considered whether to sell the Tucson property or to be absentee landlords again.

The Cases made another trip to California. They called on Dr. Rockwell D. Hunt, who was the president-emeritus of the

179

Conference of California Historical Societies at Stockton. He had conceived the California History Foundation at the University of the Pacific, and Leland drew him out on his vision of the foundation and his ideas for it.

Leland and Joan made their decision about their property: They would keep their home in Tucson and find an apartment in Stockton. As the next years went by, this proved to be a pivotal decision. The value of the property increased exponentially over the next 20 years and was a key to their financial security, as well as to their abilities to do things for institutions in which they believed.

Where The Westerners was concerned, Leland had a strong, double-edged sense of history. First, of course, was his personal interest in western history. Second was his concern for the history of The Westerners. He approached Lawrence Towner, Librarian of the Newberry Library in Chicago and raised the subject with him of the Chicago Corral depositing their materials there—their Brand Books and other printed items and their records.

Towner studied the matter, and in early 1964 he wrote an official letter to Don Russell (at Leland's suggestion) extending to the Chicago Westerners an invitation to make the Newberry their official archival depository. "Since the Newberry already has the papers of your co-founder, the late Elmo Scott Watson," he wrote, "and since, with the addition of the Everett D. Graff Collection, we became one of a few very great libraries in western Americana, the designation of the Newberry as your archival depository seems quite logical."

This initiative of Leland's opened the door for the Newberry to become a serious collector of the publications of The Westerners, and they have been receiving Westerner material from a number of corrals ever since. The University of Arizona now does the same, and several other libraries. Some, like Arizona, are pleased to receive any Westerner material they find.

In a letter Leland wrote to Roy Dunne, with King Features Syndicate in Chicago and a member of the Chicago Corral, Leland cited recent Westerner meetings he had attended at Tucson and at Stockton: "There is a vitality about/within this organization that never fails to impress me. As in setting up a magazine staff, the No. 1 problem is getting the right personnel. Do that—and there's power. I get a heavy charge out of setting up situations which draw in punchy people, then watching them achieve."

Does this simple statement explain why Leland did not become more intimately involved with Friends of the Middle Border? He had drafted the original concept and even had considered giving up his editorial career to work at Mitchell to build the institution. Having stayed with journalism, he never again took FMB into his own hands. Although he offered many suggestions and contributions, he did so always as an outside advisor.

On June 1, 1965, Leland officially retired from the Methodist Publishing House.

The Association of Methodist Historical Societies created a new regional entity for the western United States, which they called the Western Jurisdiction Historical Association. Leland attended the organizational meeting in Denver. Walter Boigegrain of Spokane was the able chairman. Leland proposed they institute a newsletter, and had already titled it, *Wesley Rides West*. A line drawing of a man on horseback would be its logo, done by a Chicago artist friend.

181

In the next couple of years Leland worked closely with Boigegrain, supporting his efforts with his knowledge of the workings of the church and his attitude as a layman willing to help. "We have exploded the tight little self-perpetuating history group and made it open to everyone," he said after the Western Jurisdictional Association was well started.

The Macmillan Company informed Leland in mid-1965 that they were discontinuing *Editing the Day's News*. The book had been a prominent text of the editing profession for over 40 years; it had even appeared in a Korean edition. But it was no longer the leader; an entirely new text was needed, and they had asked Professor Floyd Baskette at Colorado to write a new one. End of an era in education for journalism, and a new one beginning with an author that Leland himself had brought into the picture.

Leland planned carefully his departure from the Chicago scene and the move to the West. He did a round of visits and lunches and dinners to bid adieu to friendships that spanned 35 years in the Windy City.

Leland had become quite taken with the idea of a separate publication of his bibliography of early Methodist works, and he asked Ellen Blanchard if she could finish the still-formidable job of the compilation. This was quite a thing to ask. First of all, a lot of work was necessary to get it ready for publication; they both knew that. Second, Ellen had three young children and herself to support; she needed an income, and there was no money for this.

Ellen told Leland she would do the work if her name were included as his collaborator on the study. To be sure, she had worked under Leland's direction, but she had worked with skill, persistence, imagination and initiative, and these qualities were responsible for a good share of what had been produced. She had a few publishing credits in her *curriculum vitae*, and this would be a very helpful scholarly addition.

Leland rejected the idea completely. In confidence he told a couple of his colleagues about it: can you imagine her asking a thing like that? A research assistant asking to share in the credits of a scholarly work?

It reveals an interesting side of Leland Case and his times. The world of scholarship, even in the 1960s, was largely a man's world, especially in the church. Leland was the consumate professional. He was gallant and considerate with women, thanking receptionists, secretaries, librarians, and the many women who helped make his work possible. He took a sincere interest in the lives and careers of the women who worked for him, like May Aaberg and Ellen Blanchard. There was always a note of old-world courtesy. But in his professional dealings, with his peers, with scholars or publishers or university or church colleagues, one senses that women took second place in Leland's world, that the world of scholarship, religion and public affairs basically belonged to men.

This was classical in nature, rather than pernicious or sexist. He lived in the era that bridged two attitudes. That he couldn't see Ellen's point of view, or the merit of her offer, was a part of the old era, and rightly or wrongly he did not make the adjustment.

It is to Ellen's credit that she did not turn on her heel and walk away. She stayed, and she helped make an orderly transition to his new career at the University of the Pacific. She remained a good friend. And she found a new man to share in her life, the Rev. Hughes Morris, who became her husband and a father to her three children. They moved to North Platte, Nebraska, and it was a very happy marriage.

In Stockton, Leland and Joan settled into a pleasant, airy apartment on the second floor of a new building, with a view—Leland pointed out—not of craggy mountain ranges as they had in Tucson, but of five rugged oak trees.

They kept up their correspondence with Laura Fraser, in Connecticut. She suffered with severe spinal problems, but her spirit was remarkable, bright as ever. Leland had her named an honorary member of the Jedediah Smith Society in Stockton. For the Society's annual rendezvous that year she sent them a set of enlarged photographs of her American history panels at the library at West Point, which included her portrait of Jedediah Smith.

The position at the University of the Pacific was intended to be part time. Leland made of it several full-time jobs. He was Director of the California History Foundation, and he, Coke Wood and President Burns worked together to upgrade the foundation considerably. They developed new sources of funding for it, and eventually it was renamed The Holt-Atherton Center for Western Historical Studies.

As editor of the publication of the California History Foundation, *The Pacific Historian,* Leland did a thorough job of revamping what his friend Ray Billington and others thought of as a stodgy quarterly. He put together an advisory board, with the aim of having the magazine cover the west coast from Mexico to Alaska and Hawaii. He enlisted the best men he knew or knew of for this board, turning for instance to his old friend from *Revista Rotaria* days, Manolo Hinojosa, who was now editing an encyclopedia in Mexico. Billington commented to Leland, "You have attracted some first-rate articles; you have injected warmth and intimacy into the columns; and you have achieved a layout that is both attractive and enticing. Congratulations."

Putting the Stuart library collection on a better footing was one of the challenges of the job. There was also the Rockwell D. Hunt collection to catalogue and organize, the books of the founder of the California History Foundation. Leland began to steer into the library materials of all sorts related to the West. He brought in, in his first year there, almost 200 of his own volumes on Western Americana, and he urged friends all over the country to do the same. In fact, a few months before he would have suggested that almost anything of Western interest be given to Friends of the Middle Border, but he recognized that some things were more appropriate for the library at the University of the Pacific.

In agreement with Dr. Burns and related to the new Western Jurisdiction Historical Association of the Methodist Church, he greatly augmented the Methodist historical materials in the library, including some 700 books of his own. He also donated things he had picked up during his years with the Methodist Publishing House: a brick he had brought home from the rectory of Samuel Wesley at Epworth, England, where John and Charles Wesley had grown up; a brick from the home in England of Francis Asbury, one of the key figures of early Methodism in America; and one from the residence in Virginia where Asbury had held the first Methodist conference west of the Allegheney Mountains in 1788.

The Jedediah Strong Smith Society, founded at the University of the Pacific at Leland's suggestion, was another focus of energy. Dozens of letters went out in a search for Jed Smith memorabilia and archival material. The aim was to have as complete a reference collection on Smith as possible. From all over the country Leland solicited, if not originals, then microfilm and photocopies of Smith letters, diaries, contracts, and related newspaper clippings. One of the most productive of these probes was in the foreign ministry of Mexico. Jed Smith had violated Mexican-Spanish California territory in his westward push; from Mexican archives came a letter from Jed Smith's youngest brother Austin to a brother in Ohio describing Jed's death at the hands of Indians, a rare find.

The work in Stockton was interrupted by a most welcome event in Washington. Through the efforts of many who appreciated the life of Francis Case, a new bridge in the interstate highway system over the Washington Channel and in sight of the Jefferson Memorial was named for him, in a ceremony that took place in May of 1966.

Leland and Joan travelled to Washington for the dedication. Myrle Case and her daughter Jane were there, and Lois and Phil Saunders, and May Aaberg. The U.S. Army Band and an armed forces joint color guard set the tone of the affair. The entire congressional delegation of South Dakota took part: Congressmen E.Y. Berry, and Benjamin Reifel and Senator Karl Mundt made speeches, and Senator George McGovern made the dedicatory address.

Leland wrote in a letter the thoughts that went through his mind that day. "Somehow, as I sat there and absorbed — I felt much easier. Ever since that fateful morning when the doctor told me his efforts at resuscitation had been ineffective, I have had inner tensions. Francis and I were both too busy. We knew it. We talked about it. We should have taken more time to be brothers. I, personally, felt very much this way, that my work being less important I should have cut loose somehow to have given him the morale factor he needed. But there at the dedication, my emotions caught up with my mind — which has been saying, what is, IS."

In June, Leland and Joan took a long anticipated trip to the Orient: to Hawaii, to Hong Kong, to Japan and the Philippines. They visited with Carlos P. Romulo, who after a distinguished career as a soldier and statesman was serving as President of the University of the Philippines and had been Leland's friend since his days at *The Rotarian*.

In Honolulu they had a chance to spend a few days with Leland's niece Marilyn Sunderman, who had made her home there and was enjoying a flourishing career as an artist. Her studio was at the Hilton Hawaiian Village Hotel which at that time was the largest hotel in the world. Her studio was in the center of the lobby.

Leland was like a second father to Marilyn. Over the years he had been a help to her in many ways. She asked him if she could do a portrait of him. He was pleased, and agreed to pose for her.

Years later she told me two things about that portrait. In painting her uncle, what particularly interested Marilyn was the quality of his skin—so delicate and translucent. It was quite an experience for her to paint skin like that, and she positioned him with his hands in view to make the most of what she saw.

The portrait hung, unframed, in Leland's study in Tucson for several years. Then she received a letter from Uncle Leland asking her advice about framing it. He had an antique western frame that he was particularly proud of, he said, and it happened to be a few inches too short for the portrait. Which should

187

General Carlos P. Romulo, President of the University of the Philippines, addresses guests at luncheon he hosted for Leland and Joan in Manilla in 1966

I do, he asked her—cut off some of the painting at the top or cut off some at the bottom? Marilyn thought about how to answer him. Then she wrote to her uncle in this manner: "I am so thrilled with your recent manuscript. I intend to print it on some wonderful paper that I have saved for something special. The only problem is that I have not quite enough paper for the text. Which would you advise—should I leave off the first chapter or should I leave off the last chapter?"

Uncle Leland got the point. He had the portrait framed properly. It hangs in the Dakota Art Gallery at Friends of the Middle Border, and it is reproduced for the fronticepiece of this volume.

At Leland's instigation, Marilyn was awarded the Honorary Doctor of Fine Arts degree by Dakota Wesleyan University.

In Stockton there was much that could be developed by a busy mind for the Westerners Foundation, headquartered there at the college. Glen Price, whom Phil Danielson hired to develop the Foundation, had left to earn a doctorate by the time Leland arrived. Activity at the Foundation was nonexistent; it was barely "a face on the barroom floor," Leland said. Here Phil Danielson supported Leland in breathing life into the organization again.

The ferment of interest in western history, typified by the growth of The Westerners, had produced the beginnings of the Western History Association in the fall of 1961. John Alexander Carroll and John Porter Bloom, two young history professionals, had started it. Ray Billington, who was highly respected in this field, had been a force in its development. Billington knew that men of The Westerners had played a vital part in the creation of the Association; they had imparted an aura of informality to it that balanced significantly the academic tendency to stuffiness that was uncharacteristic of the West itself. He and Leland worked together to keep The Westerners in the heart of the Association.

For the Western History Association's annual conference in El Paso in October of 1966, the chairman of the program committee, Doyce B. Nunis Jr., had a bright idea. Nunis was editor of the *Southern California Quarterly* at the University of Southern California. He suggested The Westerners hold a breakfast during the conference, for Westerners and anyone else who would like to attend. Leland sent a circular to all the Westerner units of which they had any knowledge, asking for an update on their doings for a roll-call at the breakfast. That breakfast turned out to be one of the best-attended events of the whole gathering.

Back in South Dakota, Frank Thompson, a retired soil consernationist expert for the government, published the results of his many years of research about the Thoen Stone mystery, under the title *The Thoen Stone, A Saga of the Black Hills*. Leland did a review of the book for the *Rapid City Journal*. The *Journal* commented on former staffer Leland D. Case, reminding the reader of Leland and Francis and their careers in journalism in Rapid City and the Black Hills.

The *Journal* pointed out that Case, in his review, understood the value of the work of Thompson, who was strictly an amateur historian; though Thompson used unorthodox methods in researching and documenting the story of the stone, the approach he used was sound, and his conclusions were appropriate. The newspaper recognized Leland's trait of taking a rough-hewn, self-taught delver-into-history as seriously as he would a degreed scholar—listening to the layman or the Western buff as readily as though he were not outside the boundaries of the history profession.

The years at the University of the Pacific were a delight to Leland—"My two-year re-entry into Academe," he called it. The two years of constructive work, the last professional employment in his career consisted of teamwork in building the history foundation, the quarterly magazine, the Jed Smith Society, and the Western and Methodist library collections.

As I study the progress he, Dr. Burns, Coke Wood, and the others made together at Stockton, I think what a pity he could not somehow have had the same experience at Dakota Wesleyan and Friends of the Middle Border.

By August 1967 Leland and Joan were back in their own home at Tucson. How lucky it was that they hadn't sold those cactus acres. Here they felt truly at home. Leland continued to edit *The Pacific Historian* for another year, working away at its prestige with first-rate articles and with his board of advisors.

His letters reflect a contentment in Tucson as in no other place. To Warren Atherton, with whom he had worked on the Foundation at the University of the Pacific and on the Jed Smith Society, he wrote, "Have you ever seen a javalina? One crossed the road just ahead of us as Joan and I were driving in the moonlight last night. And a few days ago I was close enough to rope a coyote, if I'd had a rope. Then the other day a gorgeously patterned gila monster was loitering along my path as I walked from our adobe abode to my office."

Retirement—aged 67, with his multiple careers finally behind him—smalltown editor, Medill instructor, *Paris Herald*; *The Rotarian*, for twenty years; The Methodist Publishing House consultancy and *Together* magazine for ten years; and University of the Pacific Center for Western Studies for two years. He began to look expansively around him for the things he really wanted to do—the bibliography of early American Methodist imprints, a book or two about the Black Hills, reissuing his Black Hills Guide, Jedediah Smith, Preacher Smith, and the Tuthill hanging at Spearfish, 1884 (the execution by a mob, of a young man who may have been innocent).

He contacted his good friend Charles Ferguson, now a senior editor at *Readers Digest*. Fergie! What stories might he and Fergie do together! Fergie's response was enthusiastic: let's talk about it! And in eight or ten months he'd have a book ready that he'd like Leland to look over and give him his reactions.

This interested Leland for Charles Ferguson was a fine writer. The project was one to arouse his adrenalin—its working title was *Forever Beginning: The Story of American*

191

Methodism. For years Leland had been thinking, researching, writing about the beginnings of the Methodist movement in America, and about the impact of this movement on the way America was formed and the ideas that went into this revolutionary concept of government. Fergie and he kept in touch, and Leland waited to hear more about the book.

A number of threads were coming together that stretched back over the years. The largest, more of a hawser than a thread, was The Westerners. The time at the University of the Pacific seems to have sealed a determination in Leland Case's mind about this amorphous bundle of entities which was, to his way of thinking, his own brain-child. Developing a sound, functioning organization for the Westerners, and spreading the concept across the globe, came to be the dominating theme and the highest priority on time for Leland for the next 10 years or more. As it turned out, this determination squeezed out many of the other things Leland might have accomplished.

Another of the threads was the history of the Methodist Publishing House that had been begun in 1963 through the efforts of Leland and Jimmie Pilkington. It was published in the spring of 1968. Leland got quite a shock. Author: James Pilkington. The book acknowledged considerable research done by Dr. Leland D. Case into the pre-1789 period of Methodist publishing. That research had taken him to libraries and archives in Baltimore, New York, Philadelphia and to England. Case's reaction, which he expressed to a confidant, was that this project had been conceived and worked on as a cooperative effort, and it seemed to him a betrayal that Jimmie got credit as the author.

From the Methodist Publishing House viewpoint, of course, Leland had left their employ three years before, and perhaps it was natural that his part in the book seemed of less weight to them by this time in view of the total effort.

Once Leland had swallowed his disappointment, he had full and detailed praise for the book and for its importance to the world of history and scholarship. Jimmie Pilkington remained a good friend, and they exchanged letters from time to time.

When Charles Ferguson finally sent the manuscript he had mentioned to Leland it was more than two years later. In the interval he had retired from *Readers Digest*. The book's title now was *Organizing To Beat the Devil*. Leland sat down and read the manuscript and then put his thoughts into a 44 page memo to Fergie. The whole memorandum illustrated Leland's grasp of Methodism, or at least his own layman's interpretation of Methodism and its history, and it illustrated too the ready accessibility of all this material in his head and in his adobe office. The memo also clearly detailed his talents as an editor.

Charles Ferguson had been a seasoned senior editor for the world's widest-read magazine. He must also have been a remarkably humble man and the perfect personality to absorb and profit from Case's mature editorial and historical expertise. Leland took the time to pour his mind and heart into his friend's work for two reasons. The first was that Charles was his friend; and second, this was a work of importance to the field that had absorbed him for 10 years of professional life and into which he had been born in the parsonage of his father. It was almost as though he were transferring to Fergie what he himself might have authored about the church.

The memo itself was a work of art. It opened with a reference to the Cambridge Club he and his pals had started at Dakota Wesleyan University almost 50 years before when they felt that the theology-bound students of the Oxford Club were the darlings of the faculty and were high-handing them. The motto of the Cambridge Club was now so relevant to the title of Fergie's book—Work to beat the devil! He then discussed how to get the reader truly into the book psychologically. Leland revealed his fascination with John Wesley as a man possessed by God, hewing to the power of grace in his life and the lives of his people, with the trappings of a church and its theology ranking lower in his scale of priorities.

It was as if all Leland's years of working with the printed word—whether for the reader of the daily paper in the Black Hills, for the Rotarian in Iowa or lower Manhattan, or for the Methodist wife and children in southern California or Tidewater Virginia, and how to make things relevant for each of them—were poured into this memo to help his friend bring to life the part Methodism played in the developing of his beloved country.

And Fergie's reaction? "It never occurred to me in my wildest imaginings that you would take as much time and as many pains as you did with the manuscript. Your comments are not only immensely helpful but you do me the added and inestimable favor of giving me information as well as judgement. Hence I can pore over the comments and return to them again and again as I try to put the book in shape."

Organizing To Beat the Devil was published by Doubleday in 1971. Although not widely read, it filled a need and has a respected place in the literature of the Methodist church in America.

Leland's talents were equally involved with another, even bigger project, *The Encyclopedia of World Methodism*. Before he had left the Methodist Publishing House, in 1965, he had received a letter from Bishop Nolan B. Harmon whom the church had put in charge of this landmark effort. Bishop Harmon had asked whether Leland would be on his team to create the encyclopedia. The bishop sent a preliminary list of subjects to be included in the work and asked for suggestions.

The reply was a classic of Casiana. Leland sent him his own analysis of four categories to consider for the encyclopedia. The first, in line with his own volunteer work on the Shrines and Landmarks Committee of the Methodist Church, was for proposed new Methodist historical shrines. He listed 42 of them. The second was for living Methodists of prominence, and he included 9 names as examples. Third was deceased Methodists of prominence, listing 20, some of them little known, who might well have never occurred to the editor. The fourth was possible subjects. There were 25 of these, such as the 1737 Charles Town hymnal that John Wesley had had printed by Ben Franklin's associate; Sir Francis Drake's chaplain; ceramic busts of Wesley; and Methodist architecture. So many of the items, and the people, were obscure subjects but ones that had come to his attention in his years of digging for stories in Europe and America—things and people who had made special contributions; many had been subjects for articles in *Together* magazine.

Perhaps it's true of many of us that when we step back from the burden of a career, of being in charge, all that we have done over the years is free to flower. It seems so with Leland Case. For Bishop Harmon he set out to enhance this effort, putting himself at the service of the other man, for the common good. This happened time and time again in his retirement years.

Harmon sent him a list of items to research and to write about. Leland offered to "add a few as they come to my attention." He cited, for instance, Gabriel Poillon Disosway, a New

York merchant and one of the founders of Randoplph-Macon College. He was instrumental in publishing a letter about Indians in 1833, which historian Ray Billington claimed had made U.S. history by jarring Americans from their lethargy and setting in motion the train of events that added the Pacific Northwest to the Union. This kind of cross-career referencing that was second nature to Case was invaluable to Bishop Harmon's work.

The work on the encyclopedia occupied months of Leland's time in the next couple of years. Sometimes life's little problems would intervene. He wrote to Harmon at one point, "As one allergic to alibis, I am in a strange position. But without going into details on such matters as a break in my water main, a sewage-line stoppage, an overhead attack of termites in our kitchen, a renter who left with the financial details unadjusted, two visiting delegations from colleges interested in prospects of a considerable tract of land as a contribution on an annuity basis, an infected tooth which suddenly flared and required extraction, a brother-in-law up north hospitalized with a terminal illness, an aunt hospitalized here who requires frequent visits, floods of refugees (old friends) fleeing from northern tundras — well, without further particulars I trust that you understand that these weeks have been disruptive of plans for leaping atop your assignments. I apologize."

And of course, the Cases were enjoying retirement, where such interruptions can become more the rule than the exception, one of the luxuries that the paid professional always needs to understand in the volunteer retired person, no matter how professional the volunteer may be.

I don't know whether others of the encyclopedia team were as bullish on the human-interest side of this encyclopedia, but

196

Case kept up a stream of suggestions to Bishop Harmon to enhance that side of it. "Which reminds me," he wrote at one point,
"Schultz, creator of the Peanuts cartoon, is now a Methodist,
I've been told. A note on him would help broaden the scope—
and interest." And his concern for product over personality was
repeated—"Do not hesitate one split second to use your editorial judgement on what I send. You are the editor!"

The *Encyclopedia of World Methodism* was published by
the Methodist Publishing House, Nashville, Tennessee in 1974.

Bishop Harmon was one of the few people I've come
across in all of Leland's friendships and professional contacts with whom he never got on a first-name basis. Whether
Harmon just wasn't that type or whether the relationship remained strictly business, is a good question. It was uncharacteristic of Leland Case.

CHAPTER IX
The Leland D. Case Library
for Western Historical Studies

Leland's vast files of correspondence demonstrate that from the time he left the University of the Pacific, late in 1967, until 1981, the most time-consuming interest and labor of his life concerned The Westerners. Other concerns were there, certainly, but for sheer commitment and effort, Westerners led the field.

Westerners to Leland was "western" history, it was organization, and it was people. Leland held to the same general definition of "western" that most of the rest of us do, but in a more philosophical mood he took as one of the major delineators of "western" the term "frontier." "Frontier," Leland said, was derived from the Latin *frontera*, or "forehead." To him the word suggested resolute courage and the aggressive advance of a new and complex culture upon a more simple one. The frontier, for him, was where two cultures meet.

For example, Leland was happy to find rationale for Westerner interest in Philadelphia, since he considered it not only a fascination with the far west, but to west of the Alleghenies or even west of the Delaware. Others have taken the same approach. In his series on the Sackett family, the late Louis L'Amour wrote a great book about crossing the western frontier of the Appalachian range. Leland also liked to draw for Europeans the comparison between Julius Caesar and George Custer. Both were soldiers and commanders, and both moved against what to them were barbarians, "lesser breeds without the law," for political and economic reasons. Leland hoped someone would develop this point, but I have no idea whether anyone ever has done so. Also Leland, like Zane Grey, could find "western" material in Australia, where the advance of one culture upon another is as clearly defined as in the United States.

Leland felt that isolated groups of Westerners needed to feed and encourage, share, and relate to each other. He felt that some sort of structure or organization like the Westerners Foundation was necessary for the movement to prosper. He was not at all alone in this since the idea can be traced back to members of the Chicago Corral sharing their brand book with the budding group in Denver. In the 1970s, many thoughtful Westerners were thinking along similar lines. Ray Billington was one. Erl Ellis, an attorney who had helped start the Denver Posse and gave it years of service, was all for it. Phil Danielson had put his money behind the conviction of creating the Westerner Foundation.

Danielson later said, "My real interest has been to back Leland's cause" for, although he often disagreed with Leland, he felt there was no one on the horizon with Leland's grasp of the true nature of The Westerners or of where it ought to be headed. Don Russell of Chicago came to feel a national network was important, and he edited the first edition of the *Buckskin Bulletin*. Al Larson of Laramie was a strong supporter, as were Paul Galleher of Arthur H. Clark publishers and Joe Rosa of London. As Leland's crusade to develop more corrals and to build a stronger organization went on, appreciation for what he was doing grew wider and deeper.

Then there were people who didn't care, those whose personalities clashed with Leland's and those who strongly opposed any kind of organization. Some derided Leland for trying to make Westerners into a copy of Rotary. Some had no interest in anyone doing anything outside their own group. Some still feel this way.

Leland found himself refining and rearticulating his concept over and over again through the years. His "western" sense of the virtues of self-reliance and independence told him that corral units should be self-governing and self-determining, whereas his 20 years of experience with Rotary told him that umbrella guidelines were important. Guidelines for this assortment of totally autonomous units, of course, would have to be far different from guidelines for the relatively tightly-structured Rotary movement.

For example, there was the question of membership for women in The Westerners. When the New York corral was founded in 1952, the fifth in the history of the organization, Nebraska-born author Mari Sandoz was a charter member. No one would have dared deny this widely-known and highly-respected scholar a place in the young world of Westerners. Nevertheless, for years Leland said, before and after the New York corral began, that The Westerners was mostly a men's group. One of his convictions was that women tend to make a corral a social club, unless they are real pros like Mari Sandoz. By the mid-1970s Leland was promoting co-ed corrals. For many of the groups it was a matter of survival. It is no secret that his "druthers" would have been, however, for male camaraderie. Dayton W. Canaday, director of the South Dakota State Historical Society, was the one who coined the phrase "sidesaddlers" for woman members. Leland always added, when referring to the term, that you should smile when you said it.

To Leland, one of the most important elements of a successful organization was communication. His much-loved friend Elmo Scott Watson had started the Chicago Westerners *Brand Book* almost in the same breath with which they had started

The Westerners itself. In some ways it had served as a communications medium for all Westerners.

In 1960, at the College of the Pacific, as it was called until 1961, the Westerners Foundation issued Volume I, Number 1 of *Buckskin Bulletin*, edited by Don Russell, "published occasionally." It carried a register of units: Chicago Corral, Denver Posse, Los Angeles Corral, St. Louis Corral (inactive at the time), New York Posse, Tucson Corral, Wyoming Corral, Black Hills Corral, English Westerners Society, Potomac Corral, Kansas City Posse, Spokane Corral, French Corral, Stockton Corral, German Corral, Swedish Corral and the Phoenix Corral, whose founding was the lead article in the edition.

"Occasionally" was certainly how it was published. The next issue did not appear until the fall of 1968. It offered a Certificate of Registration to any qualifying outfit and would supply a "genyouwine Buckskin with the data imprinted thereon" for $35. The mailing address was the postal route of Leland Case's cactus acres.

The third edition of *Buckskin Bulletin* was dated Autumn 1969. This one marked the point at which Leland made a serious commitment to put his shoulder to the Westerner wheel.

Home for Joan and Leland was in Tucson. He had his comfortable surroundings, his convenient adobe study or office, his church and Rotary Club, a growing list of friends, and the Tucson Corral, which he had founded with interested friends in 1953. He was convinced by now that the Westerners as a network of autonomous corrals would prosper if it were properly promoted. He called on the city manager, the Chamber of Commerce, the president of the University of Arizona, the arts and culture groups, the Arizona Historical Society, and leaders of private business and industry. A whole list of these people responded to his request for letters urging The Westerners to locate their headquarters in Tucson.

The next issue of *Buckskin Bulletin*, Volume IV, Number 1, appeared early in 1970, and announced the move of the Westerners Foundation to Tucson. The Foundation had become Westerners International. It was conveniently located near the University of Arizona in the balcony of a branch of the Southern Arizona Bank (now the First Interstate Bank of Arizona). This ample, airy space was given rent-free to Westerners until mid-1977, when the building was demolished in favor of a drive-in hamburger haven. This edition of the *Bulletin* was edited by *Tucson Daily Citizen* columnist Don Schellie, of the Tucson Corral. The edition contains fourteen "business card" advertisements.

From then on, the *Bulletin* came out at least three times a year, and often four. Advertising mostly by book publishers and dealers, with few courtesy ads, was carrying the cost of publication. Although Don Schellie could not continue as editor, and a series of editors came along, the paper came out with regularity.

Leland Case's hand can be seen in much of it. He instituted the Living Legend feature in the fall of 1970 (Volume V, Number 1). The first Legend, un- numbered, was Leland's own salute to John G. Neihardt, Nebraska's Poet Laureate and one of those at the organizing meeting of The Westerners in Evanston in 1944. The cavalcade of Living Legends has proceeded down the years, and has told of people who have built The Westerners or have exemplified the Westerner spirit. There have been 33 Living Legends published, as this book goes to press.

Leland and Joan got away to Europe in the summer of 1971. It was a happy three weeks around the continent by Eurorail

Pass—Amsterdam, a West German boat down the Danube, Italy, Geneva—and 10 days poking into Lafayette's history. They visited the Count Rene de Chambrun, of the Lafayette family, whose uncle Leland had gotten to know in his *Paris Herald* days. Leland pursued Lafayette's trail to Olmutz, now part of Czechoslovakia, where the Marquis had been imprisoned for five years. Here, with a Czech friend, Leland was snapping photographs when a woman decided he was a Western spy and called the police. Leland was carted off to jail, and it took his friend several hours to get him out.

Now well settled into Tucson, Leland picked up another thread from the past. He reinstituted his membership in the Masonic Order. Having resigned from the Macalester lodge in 1932, he affiliated himself in 1969 with Jerusalem Daylight Lodge No. 66 in Tucson. He remained in good standing with the Masons for the rest of his life. He did some study of the order, writing away for books and pamphlets on various phases of Masonry.

In 1972, Leland received a letter from Dean Krakel at the Cowboy Hall of Fame. Krakel reported in the letter his struggle for almost 10 years to finance and create a memorial to the work of James Earl Fraser and Laura, at the Hall. The struggle had involved bringing to the Hall the great old original plaster statue of *The End of the Trail*, which after the Panama-Pacific Exposition of 1915 had migrated to the small California town of Visalia. To gain this plaster original, Krakel had to provide Visalia with a full-sized bronze *End of the Trail*, at immense cost. Then he had to restore the original and create for it a building on the grounds of the Hall.

There he also gathered many plaster original works of both James and Laura, including the Oklahoma Run frieze which

203

had caught his attention in the first place. All of this represented over a million dollars, Krakel's letter said. And to think that this all began, he told Leland, with your letter in 1962 urging me to see the Oklahoma frieze in Laura's studio. Krakel sent to Leland a small bronze version of *The End of the Trail* "in gratitude for all you have done and are doing to preserve our heritage."

The emblem of The Westerners has been the buffalo skull, ever since Elmo Scott Watson had included one crudely drawn on the first mimeographed issue of the *Chicago Brand Book*. John Jameson, one of the early members in Chicago, recalled for Leland the origin of the name of the skull—"Old Joe." It happened back in 1956 or '57, he said, when he was sheriff of the Chicago Corral. Leland, at a meeting, suggested they name the buffalo skull which had been contributed to them by the superintendent of Yellowstone National Park. He scribbled a note to Jameson saying his idea for the name came from the old singsong doggerel:

> Joe, Joe broke his toe
> riding on a buffalo.

And Old Joe it's been ever since.

As an indication of how seriously Leland took this work with The Westerners, consider his friend from *Rotarian* days, Hal Cooley. Hal for years edited *Chinorama Magazine* for the Kennecott Copper Company near Silver City, New Mexico, where he belonged to the Westerner unit there. When he retired and settled in nearby Deming, Leland made a serious proposition—that he and his wife Nynah move to Tucson and take on *Buckskin Bulletin*. Of course the salary and perks would have been the same as Leland's—satisfaction in doing the job.

Hal and Nynah were happy where they were. He edited the *Bulletin* from his Deming home, for a few months, but he turned to other pursuits that did not subject him to pressures from Leland Case.

In his development of a coordinating body for The Westerners, Leland instituted regular meetings of the board of directors each year at the Western History Association conferences. He served as president of Westerners during this transition period. He built an executive committee of men— and eventually including women—who lived within an hour or two's drive from Tucson, a committee that met every other month and hammered out the affairs of the organization.

Now, for the first time, Westerners had an organizational structure that was functioning year round. The office on the balcony at the Southern Arizona Bank became a place known to readers of the *Buckskin Bulletin* and to those who corresponded with the "home ranch." In the office was a roster of volunteers who manned it each morning of the business week and a visitor's register signed by Westerners who dropped in for a chat. These were all touches that Leland built into the Westerners' operation in Tucson.

In 1973, the thirtieth year of Westerners, Don Russell became president of the international organization. Leland Case was given the title of President Emeritus and Keeper of the Pitchfork—in recognition of his continuing role in prodding matters along. From that time on, the board of Westerners International selected an outstanding Westerner from somewhere in the network to serve as international president. The work load was carried by the "home ranch" and executive committee, but the president could plan an agenda for his year that reflected his perspective on affairs of the organization from a wider view than that of Tucson.

Continually in the '70s Leland told friends that he was determined to work his way out of the leadership in Westerners and turn it over to others. In creating this Executive Committee he delegated tasks to those he enlisted into service, but he was right there with fresh ideas and repeated old ones, calling on his experience of Rotary and Friends of the Middle Border and his magazine career to formulate sound principles of organization. Some of those have become legends—the three C's of Communication, Coordination, and Cooperation, for instance.

Two of his favorites were the Biblical quotation, "And there arose a pharaoh who knew not Joseph" for the transitory nature of agreements not on paper; and from *Mrs. Minever*, the English war-time novel by Jan Struther, who wrote that history was like a rear-view mirror in an automobile—"You can

Don Russell, George Virgines, Leland Case and Fred Hackett at the Chicago Corral "founders' night" 1974

206

Don Russell with the Chicago Corral's emblem

not successfully navigate the future unless you keep always framed beside it a small clear image of the past."

There was a drawback to Leland's concentrating so hard on The Westerners. It was that his thinking sometimes became too codified, too fixed, for outside thoughts to penetrate. For example, George Chalfont, a rancher and businessman in Ukiah, on the northern California coast, reported the formation of The Redwoods Coast Outpost of Westerners. This group of men, spreading from the Golden Gate to the Oregon border, surely one of God's choicest stretches of seaside geography, associated themselves into a corral—though shunning that name in favor of "outpost." They met in various locations and had a lively, productive fellowship. But Leland's mind fastened onto the place-name Ukiah. So despite repeated suggestions from

Chalfont, and a growing affectionate camaraderie between the two men, it was the Ukiah Corral in Westerner correspondence and in the *Buckskin Bulletin* for as long as it was active and Leland Case was around. It was not what they wished to be called, and they did not call themselves that.

A similar thing happened in Colorado, and the reactions were more drastic. In 1974, a group of folks for whom there was no room in the Denver Posse decided to start another corral in the Denver area. They looked to Westerners International to supply guidance, and Leland and the "home ranch" workers leaned forward to help. They wished to be known as the Colorado Corral. John Albright, the acting secretary of the new group, lived in the Denver suburb of Littleton. Leland, with the volunteers at the Westerner office following his lead, tabbed it as the Littleton corral. John Albright wrote that they seemed to have a serious communication problem. They wished to be known as the Colorado Corral, and Littleton was a misnomer, so they requested a change.

The group announced the date of their first formal meeting, and Leland rushed a registration certificate, duly signed by numerous WI officers, including the then president, Denver Posse member Erl Ellis, made out to the Littleton Corral. By return mail their sheriff sent the certificate back. "Since you seem unable to insert us into the name and location we desire," he wrote, "I think it best if we amicably part our ways. I would appreciate no further correspondence until after I leave office. I certainly see nothing wrong with the Westerners International movement, but the whole manner in which our group has been approached has been little more than condescending and insulting."

Eventually the breech was healed, and today the Colorado Corral based in Denver is a going concern and maintains its tie with Westerners International.

Perhaps these conflicts arose out of the speed with which Leland's mind worked, the concentration he put into his efforts, and the preoccupation which kept him from hearing what others said to him.

Another of the concepts that Leland wrestled into being in those formative days of 1969 and '70 was the awards program. Phil Danielson was interested in setting up a competition that would encourage people to produce higher quality talks at corrals. He had more faith in the durability of the University of the Pacific than he had in the future of Westerners, and so he executed an agreement with the university that the interest income on a $5000 natural gas pipeline bond would go to Leland Case, during his lifetime, for prize money for the best talks or papers presented to corrals. At Leland's demise the bond and its interest would become the property of the university.

The first series of awards was announced during the Westerner breakfast at the Western History Association conference in Reno in the fall of 1970. This ceremony gave a fresh point of interest to the breakfast.

Twice in the next years when the awards did not go as he felt they should, Danielson threatened to eliminate the whole program. Leland managed to dissuade him and to keep the concept going. Finally Leland was able to sell Danielson on making his pipeline bond the property of The Westerners, with a sunset clause in favor of the University of the Pacific in case Westerners International went out of business.

Leland felt there should be prizes for other achievements in addition to the Danielson awards—a prize for corral activities that stimulated their communities to a greater interest in history, and prizes for books by members of Westerners. He tried various avenues to raise the endowment funds for these awards, but finally he and Joan decided they should better give the money themselves. The Cases gave a $5000 New York Telephone Company bond the interest of which would support what he called "Co-Founders Awards," in tribute to Elmo Scott Watson working beside him to get Westerners off the ground.

Over the years the awards program has grown, and money to support it has come, but it all started with Leland Case and Phil Danielson.

As the 1970s wore along, two other interests took a good bit of Leland's attention. One was Friends of the Middle Border, which in his mind always was the starting point for The Westerners, and the other was the disposition of his personal library.

I have spent a lot of time and a number of paragraphs of this book in thought about Friends of the Middle Border and how Leland related to it over the years. We have great quantities of material in his own papers about FMB; but if we could still sift through the files back in College Hall that were destroyed by the fire of 1955 would we learn something more about his relationship to FMB?

Before Leland was through, he had put many thousands of dollars into Friends of the Middle Border—in participating in building-fund drives, in paying for improvements and repairs to their buildings, in long-term financial arrangements, in scholarship endowments—almost always as a challenge to the Friends

210

*Friends of the Middle Border's Pioneer Museum, Mitchell, SD—main entrance
(courtesy of Friends of the Middle Border)*

and their leadership to match what he was giving. So few people
picked up his challenges. Certainly notes of bitterness crept in,
although in the main he addressed the lost opportunities and
moved on. He certainly felt keenly that no one picked up open-
ings he created for them, with Harvey Dunn, James Earle Fraser,
Laura Gardin Fraser, Charles Hargens, the Kresge Foundation,
people who could open doors to money, to collections of papers, to art treasures.

He saw Friends of the Middle Border not only as a museum, not only as a "living history" exposition—the new kind
of museum that was being pioneered by people like Henry Ford
at Greenfield Village. But he saw it, too, as a research and
study facility, a resource for serious study of the West. He had
that idea before Thomas Gilcrease created the great Gilcrease
Institute of American History and Art, before the National
Cowboy Hall of Fame & Western Heritage Center. He watched

211

the State University at Brookings, north of Mitchell, accept Harvey Dunn's station-wagon load of paintings and go state-wide with the womens' clubs to build a whole art center around them. He watched Augustana College at Sioux Falls raise in a few months $155,000 to launch their Center for Western Studies in the early '70s.

And as these things roll off my word processor, I keep thinking—if Friends of the Middle Border meant so much to him, which it most certainly did, why did he not do for it what he did for Westerners ?

It's not that he raised a lot of money for Westerners—he gave a $5000 bond, following Danielson's lead; he oversaw the creation of an endowment fund, and hoped he could interest several people to give substantial sums to it, although they did not. He wanted to see one of us really run with the idea of a building of our own, but there was no one who responded to that size of a project. He did not, perhaps surprisingly, include The Westerners in his will.

His main contribution to Westerners was the hard work to develop the corrals and the organization to serve them. The persistent work of building and promoting. In this, he was "it." He took full responsibility for it. It was his task that he had set himself to do. Suppose he had done that for Friends of the Middle Border? In this case, it seems he had accepted that someone else would be "it," and that he would exhort from the sidelines. Was FMB too small a canvas for him to paint on? Is that why he invested all that time and energy and skill in The Westerners?

The progress of Friends of the Middle Border depended so much on who they had as executive director. The high point had been during the tenure of Leonard Jennewein, who com-

212

bined the talents of a sound academic program with the art of making much out of little resources.

The other key to the Friends was the caliber of volunteers who put time and effort into it. Occasionally there were those who would intelligently pursue people who had money that might be given to FMB or gifts in kind.

One such gift was an abandoned rural railway station, from Dimock, down the Milwaukee Line from Mitchell, complete with a section of track and hand- operated signal tower. Another was the Louis Beckwith house, built in 1886; Beckwith was one of the first residents of the town of Mitchell, and was one of the two men who created the now-famous Mitchell Corn Palace, which is the principle tourist attraction of the town.

Then the Friends acquired an 1885 one-room schoolhouse and a rural church of 1909. A great deal of care and money went into the restoration of these buildings, and the result is a fine historic village campus for FMB, together with the main buildings that house the various collections.

For Leland, the steady contact with Friends of the Middle Border, and Dakota Wesleyan as well, was Gordon Rollins. In the mid-'70s Gordon resigned his position as business manager of DWU and took on the work of raising money for the college—development, it is called today. Gordon was an astute fund raiser. He maintained contact and friendship with Leland and Joan Case through thick and thin. When Leland felt things at FMB were going badly, Rollins would agree but would hold out a positive thought for Leland to build on. His letters proposing ways for Leland and Joan to help the college are classics of good fund-raising, always indicating a fresh turn to take or opportunity to serve.

I think he learned from his relationship with Leland, also.

At one point, when matters seemed at a low ebb, Leland said to him, "Too often Dakota Wesleyan says 'gimme' where the donor wants to hear 'lemme.'" Between them, Case and Rollins worked at the finances of Friends of the Middle Border, and plotted how to establish an endowment fund to sustain it.

The investment of time and energy that Leland made in the Westerner movement was a clear commitment for him, and it took precedence over other things he might have been doing with his life. "I find myself the surer," he wrote to a friend in 1976, "that getting active corrals going around this minor planet of ours is a fairly important thing. Once we get to 100, maybe the next thing is to look after the internal health of those we have."

In the fall of 1973, Leland Sonnichsen, whom Case loved to call "my nominal cousin" on the strength of their common first names, wrote to decline to serve longer on the Executive Committee of Westerners International and as chairman of WI's committee for annual awards. Sonnichsen was about the same age as Case. He was at the time editor of publications for the Arizona Historical Society, after a successful career in teaching English at what is now the University of Texas at El Paso. He was 72, life was moving on, and he had a series of books in mind that he had set himself to produce. He felt that judging others' works and editing others' writings, was less and less his task. Leave that to those who felt so inclined.

Sonnichsen and Case were friends, of course, and contemporaries and were members of the Tucson Literary Club together. Both were lifelong Western afficionados and professional men. It is in the paths they took or in their use of their talents that I like to compare the two Lelands. Case had books he wanted to write, things he wanted to explore, areas he longed to research. But he was also a born promoter and developer. He had taken The Westerners on as a work to complete—to put it on a sound footing and to see it prosper. Other things that he wanted to do simply took a back seat.

And from that year–1973–until his death in 1991, Leland Sonnichsen has had published 13 books (with three more on the way), 26 articles in journals and magazines, and 24 other offerings, such as chapters in books or prefaces to the works of others. As he said of Leland Case, "I hope I have been of some help to him in carrying out the difficult job he has laid out for himself, but I think he understands my position." Sonnichsen had respect for Case, and Case for him.

In Leland Case's own Westerner files there are 428 separate file folders, representing 428 specific locations in which there was a thought of a corral being formed and at least some action taken. Many of them represented the work of other people. But most of the files represent at least some thought and action by Leland Case, whether it was one shot or a whole campaign lasting years. The fact that to date there have been over 130 corrals registered, even though a number of them are "in dry camp," attests to the work Leland put in on the effort.

"Dry camp," by the way, was Leland's way of saying that a corral had become inactive. He refused to concede that a corral, once established by a group of sincere people, could die.

Leland's other interest in the 1970s was his library. As a book man, editor, semihistorian, semischolar, he was proud of his books and he felt there was a value in them that should accrue to one of the institutions that had played a part in his past. His attempt to work out a Francis Case—Leonard

Jennewein—Leland Case collection for Dakota Wesleyan foundered really on his and Jennewein's inability to reach a common mind, and perhaps on a malaise at the college itself. His feeling that Friends of the Middle Border was turning out to be more of a museum than a serious research center played a big part here.

He sent selected volumes to Macalester, his alma mater, but perhaps Macalester was better endowed and financed, and with a larger library environment, to be a serious possibility for him. Black Hills State College—which had been a state teacher's college when he took a year of high school there—is where his interest began to focus. Besides, it was part of his beloved Black Hills.

Dr. M.N. Freeman, President at Black Hills, and Dr. E. Keith Jewitt, Dean of Academic Affairs, responding to a feeler that Leland put out, came to see him in Tucson in early 1973. They were armed with a dossier on the college and its surrounding environment. They wanted the library. They were just finishing a new facility, named for E.Y. Berry, who had served in Congress from the West River area of South Dakota from 1952 to 1970.

Like Leland and Francis, Berry was Iowa born, and a newspaperman. The E.Y. Berry Learning Center is a handsome three-story building providing 60,000 square feet of space, a major addition to the pleasant campus. Berry had agreed to leave his library and papers to the school, along with some money. The Learning Center would house the college library and would have a Special Collections segment that would contain his papers, the archives of the college, and the Case library if Leland decided to give it.

The college was part of the state-funded system and had an

216

enrollment of around 1500 students. There was a new dynamic librarian, Dr. Edwin Erickson, and a new professor of history, David Miller, studying for his doctorate at the University of Kansas. Both would be involved with the Case collection. The facilities that they offered appealed to Leland—the new building, the Special Collection situation, controlled access, trained supervision, and the promise that his collection would be used to develop additional history courses, especially graduate work. They also agreed with him that their professional catalog system would offer a duplicate set of the catalog of his things to the South Dakota School of Mines and Technology at Rapid City, thereby extending the use of his materials to the "metropolis" of western South Dakota.

By the spring of 1974, Leland had signed an agreement with President Freeman to give his library, together with a sum of money to provide endowment for its upkeep, to Black Hills State College. Leland was elated. BHSC was the one Liberal Arts school in western South Dakota. He turned to the task of organizing what would be called The Leland D. Case Library for Western Historical Studies. All the old vigor and organizing skills were called upon. All that he had learned in reorganizing the library at the University of the Pacific, as well as in creating *Together* Magazine with its library, archives, and research department, was poured into this task.

Whether Dr. Erickson had any idea he was to be on the receiving end of this avalanche, he soon found out. Leland wrote memoranda concerning the staff the library should have, the library committee that should oversee the staff, and how each of these should operate. He was concerned about the creation of book plates, donor plates, letterheads, application forms to gain access to the collection, admission cards, gift forms, thank-you forms, processing procedures, an accession book, and the catalog system.

The Case Library was to be, above all, functional—easy for scholars to use. To this end, its materials were organized not only by the Library of Congress system, to be compatible with any library in the United States, but also they were carded and shelved by topical categories that were based upon actual classroom use. It was clearly a study center. One would have to qualify as a serious student to obtain a Case Library Admission Card, and materials were to be studied there, in the reading room, just as in the Newberry and other special reference libraries across the country.

The library dedication date was set for April 30, 1976. Leland worked to prepare for that date at a pace anyone else would have called full time. Dr. Erickson felt the brunt of much of this. He had that handicap that some institutions suffer with—there was one secretary-typist to serve eight people like himself. He could not at all keep pace with Leland's flow of ideas and details.

As Leland worked at the founding of his library, what was becoming apparent was that Black Hills State College was a small place. Leland thought in terms of the Newberry Library and the vast resources at its command, or the Bancroft, backed up by the University of California at Berkley. Here was rural Black Hills State College that could profit hugely from the library if they could get it into operation and maintain it, and if there were the programs of study geared to use it.

Leland worked on the details of his endowment gift, to further the effectiveness of his library. He stipulated a series of prizes for college-level history studies. Then at the high school level, for the surrounding area—four Westerners Awards. They

218

were to be administered in conjunction with the Westerner corrals at Rapid City, Hot Springs and at Billings, Montana, and they were to be presented at a public function, such as the annual Black Hills History Conference sponsored by the college and the state historical society.

As the opening date neared, a stream of letters and phone calls went from Leland to Dr. Freeman and to Ed Erickson, covering details on the dedication ceremony itself, on the public promotion of it, and on printed materials to be available explaining the library, the prizes, and how to contribute materials to the collection.

Leland put on paper plans for a corps of field historians who would keep their eyes and ears open for materials to augment the library—the batch of old letters someone might find in their attic, the old newspapers stuffed in the wall to keep out the cold and found when the kitchen was renovated, priceless material that would fill out the picture of the social, political, economic history of the region.

He saw the collection in its fullest potential, and he saw it as a tremendous resource—far beyond the use to which undergraduates at BHSC, at present, would put it. Here was a mind that knew what a major research center was, working to use his own collection as the magnet to create a major center in the Black Hills. Leland knew Spearfish, its beautiful setting on the north edge of the Black Hills, and its climate. He foresaw the lure of this setting in the cool of the summer and what could be done there, in addition to the study center, with music and drama and art. It was a grand concept. It was as grand, in its own way, and as well filled-out, as his concept in 1939 had been for Friends of the Middle Border.

CHAPTER X
The End of the Trail Comes Home

The Cases made a sortie to Cape Canavaral in December, 1972. Dr. Harrison H. Schmitt, son of Leland's cousin on his mother's side of the family and a geologist with a broad scientific background, was to be launched in Apollo XVII to the moon. He was the first civilian to make the voyage. Leland felt constrained to be at the Cape, he told friends, to see that the rocket was aimed right.

What a thrill for Leland! He who, near the beginning of the century, had jostled out to South Dakota in a dusty railroad train, had delivered chickens to the neighbors in his family buggy, and who had interviewed Orville Wright and Charles Lindbergh. Schmitt and his compadres made it to the moon and back all right. He and Eugene Cernan set a record by being on the moon's surface for 75 hours. Schmitt went on to serve a term in the Senate from New Mexico.

As the day drew closer for the dedication of the library at Spearfish, Leland wrote notes to a great many of his friends. The gist of the notes was that his library would put Black Hills State College on a new footing, in the league of those that had regional historical research facilities; that he wanted the college to realize what they were about to have on campus and the importance of it; and that a letter of congratulations from his friends would underline this importance and lift the thinking of the college to a new plane.

Responses came from a wide variety of these people—from Archibald Hanna, of the Beineke Library at Yale University; Norman Cousins, editor of *Saturday Review*; Lowell Thomas;

Fred Vosburgh of *National Geographic*; Ray Billington; William Alderson, Executive Director of the American Association of State and Local History; Dean Krakel of the Cowboy Hall of Fame; Larry Pressler, Congressman from South Dakota and now Senator; John Mack Carter, who had worked for Leland on *Together* magazine and was now editor of *Good Housekeeping* magazine.

Leland also spread the word that the Case collection was just the beginning of this western historical library, and that others could contribute their material to make it grow. People responded. Bill Steen, longtime Tucson Westerner, physician and book collector, sent a selection from his library. Don Russell, pillar of the Chicago Westerners, assigned some of his.

April 30, 1976 was a day to remember at Black Hills State College—the dedication of the Leland D. Case Library for Western Historical Studies. After an invocation by the Methodist pastor in Spearfish and suitable remarks by the college president and by one of the South Dakota Regents of Education, Leland was asked to speak.

He called his address "The Splendid Obsession at Spearfish." He quoted his favorite word-picture from Jan Struther's *Mrs. Miniver*—"You can not successfully navigate the future unless you keep always framed beside it a small clear image of the past." With his friendly wit and verbal imagery, Leland traced the determination of free men in South Dakota and the Black Hills, sparked by the few who were bold to create opportunities for education. He recounted the history of Black Hills State College with a slew of little-remembered details.

And now, Leland said, with his own gift as a nucleus, they had already attracted the Mt. Rushmore Memorial Society Records, and a notable collection of maps and ornithology, a collection of 4,000 microfilmed town and county papers, and others. Leland sketched 15 or so diverse topics one could study right now at the research center—as soon as the materials had been organized—from Deadwood Dick dime novels to the project of luring the United Nations to establish its headquarters in the Black Hills, which his brother Francis had spearheaded. And he stressed the urgency of his library project. Already, he warned, libraries in great urban centers were collecting Black Hills materials to salt away in their catacombs.

Had Spearfish ever before heard anyone quote, appropriately and intelligently, not only from local historical figures, but from the words inscribed on the tomb of Sir Christopher Wren in London, from Mark Twain, *The Wall Street Journal*, Isaiah, The Venerable Bede, and Lord Bryce, all in the course of one well-constructed speech?

The college printed up copies of Leland's address, and he sent them to his list of several hundred friends and professional contacts that spanned his lifetime. It was a proud moment for him.

At Dr. Erickson's request, Leland had sent to the library an oil painting of himself and his black-and-white dog Fritz. His staff artist at *Together*, Floyd A. Johnson, had painted it for him and presented it in 1963 at the dinner honoring his service to the magazine.

As the nation began to gear up for the American Revolution Bicentennial of 1976, Leland was one of many across the country who looked for ways to use this occasion to advance the cause of history and historical preservation. He was appointed as an advisor to the original Bicentennial Commission in Washington, and he participated in the thinking of the United Methodist Church on the subject.

The End of the Trail Comes Home

As the Black Hills were always close to his heart, he gave a good bit of thought to how they should be represented in Bicentennial activities and how to take permanent advantage of national and state Bicentennial recognition. To the East Coast thirteen-original-colonies mentality, 1976 meant the bicentennial of the Declaration of Independence and the American Revolution. To the Dakotas, Wyoming and Montana it meant the Centennial of the Battle of Little Big Horn and the defeat of George Armstrong Custer.

In the Black Hills General Custer stood for more than just the Little Big Horn and American's most devastating defeat at the hands of the Indians. Custer had forever changed the history of the area by his expedition to the Hills in 1874 and the discovery of gold. That had altered the relationship of Indian to white in the area for all time, had opened the area to an influx of people, and had begun the most colorful chapter in the story of the Hills.

On visits to the Black Hills Leland raised with the Methodist pastor at Deadwood the possibility of using the Bicentennial-Centennial period as a lever to create a greater awareness of the history of the region. Deadwood had a particular appeal because of its name—the saloon where Wild Bill Hickok was murdered and the Homestake Mining Company in nearby Lead, the most productive gold mine in the United States.

Leland and others were interested in telling the story of those exciting days with more veracity and in greater depth than tourism generally gave the public. For Methodists, their church was woven into the history of the Black Hills from the earliest days of white men's exploration, prospecting and settling— Jedediah Smith, a Methodist and a man of prayer; General Custer, Hickok and many another had had Methodist affiliation.

223

THE MAN FROM THE HILLS

The Case Indian Art Collection is presented to LaGrange College in 1978. (left to right) John Lawrence, director of the college's art museum, Mrs. Case and Leland

And, Deadwood had its own bona fide Methodist martyr, Preacher Smith. Perhaps now was the time to do something dramatic about him.

Dr. Henry Hottmann had taken up the pastorate of the First United Methodist Church of Deadwood in 1972. Leland met him that year and planted with him the thought of developing a Black Hills Methodist historical society and museum. Dr. Hottmann responded, on stationary of the church subheaded "Bearing Christian Witness Since Henry Weston (Preacher) Smith 1876." A meeting was held. Dr. Hottmann found it a stimulating and productive time. Among the local people who stepped forward was Dean Nauman, who had been a pupil of Mrs. Hottmann's years before in Gettysburg, near the center of the state, and as a young man had been the first paid secretary of Friends of the Middle Border.

224

Leland helped develop an application for the historical society museum to be named a shrine of the Methodist church, and he fed the new group with materials on the national Bicentennial program. He sent an eight-page memorandum outlining the rationale for what they were doing, how to develop celebrations around their historical figures, and ten other specific examples of Methodist influence in the Black Hills. He outlined organization, finance, public relations and other aspects that ought to be taken into account.

As often happens, the folks on the spot see the needs and the solutions from their own perspective. Leland envisioned a museum; they wanted—and got—a heritage center. The vision that caught on was of a center in Western America that demonstrated how the lengthening shadow of one man, John Wesley, could penetrate even the canyons and gold creeks of the Black Hills and spread its arms to include higher education, hospitals and organizations through men and women of good will. They obtained the use of the lower floor of a former bank building right on Main Street in the heart of Deadwood, and they designed and built the center within it with their own hands, with stained glass panels, a diorama, photo blowups, display cases and lighting.

People gave artifacts, such as the silver communion vessels that Leland's sisters Carol and Joyce sent from the Hot Springs Methodist Church. Mamie Martin, the longtime friend of Leland's Aunt Edith Grannis, gave $5000, which was matched by the Deadwood Methodist Church. A great-granddaughter of Henry Weston Smith gave the money to create a stained glass window memorial to the Preacher. And the largest gift was from the Methodist church in nearby Terraville.

That church stood on land that the Homestake Mine needed for expanding their open-pit operation; they agreed with the mining company on a price for their land and gave part of the money to the new heritage center. They erected in one of its rooms a fine replica of the Terraville church, with a color photo blow-up of the magnificent view of Bob Tail Gulch that one could always see out the window as you looked toward the altar.

In 1978 The Preacher Smith Heritage Center opened, sponsored by the Black Hills Regional United Methodist Historical Society. It has been serving the region ever since, an attractive, much visited and beautifully interpretive element there. It is designated as a national shrine of Methodism, the first west of the Missouri.

Dean Nauman still speaks of creating that shrine with real pride and also with a touch of wistfulness—for he felt that Leland, once the project was launched, took all the hard work that others put into it for granted. "One pat on the back from the founder would have been good," he said many years later. "Bibliophile-supreme, dreamer and doer, Leland could have walked through the place, examining in his best Basil Rathbonese. Ah! that would have been the frosting on the cake!"

Leland's long-time interest in General Lafayette led him in divers directions. In 1825 and '26, Lafayette had been invited by the U.S. government to tour all the American states in celebration of the nation's first 50 years. That tour had stimulated many areas of the country to name a town, a street, a park or college for the Frenchman, or for his estate in France, La Grange, or for some other reference to him.

LaGrange, in western Georgia, was one of these towns, and its college too. Along about 1970, Dr. Waights G. Henry,

226

the president of LaGrange College, expressed to one of his faculty his interest in knowing something about the man in whose honor the town and college were named. Dr. Henry was a dynamo of energy and initiative, a great promoter and fund-raiser, with a lively intellect and a delightful wit. The professor he spoke to, a Frenchman and Head of his Modern Languages Department, had been at the University of the Pacific when Leland was there, and remembered Leland's considerable knowledge of Lafayette.

This bringing together of Dr. Case and Dr. Henry was like striking flint to steel to light a fire. From then on the two men and their wives not only became good friends, but they conspired to achieve some interesting things for LaGrange College and for its town. Case looked around for books and memorabilia about Lafayette that should have a place at La Grange College. He located a copy of *Lafayette in America, Day By Day* the story of the 1825 visit. He found a song written for Lafayette's tour of 1825 called "Washington's Favorite The Brave Lafayette", and sent it along.

Waights Henry thought about a suitable memorial in the town, which would bring meaning to the name of La Grange for residents and students alike. Leland told him about the full-sized statue of Lafayette at his birthplace, the Chateau Chavaniac at Le Puy, in France. The sculptor was the distinguished Ernest-Eugene Hiolle, a 19th century Frenchman. Dr. Henry put to work his talent for inspiring potential benefactors, the necessary funds were raised, and a copy of the statue was commissioned, along with a setting for it in the center of the town.

In their now constant flow of correspondence, Henry raised the subject of how to celebrate the dedication of the statue in LaGrange. Leland suggested they make it a Bicentennial event:

commission a series of paintings on the life of Lafayette; and invite Rene De Chambrun, owner of the original La Grange estate, over to speak. The ideas appealed to Dr. Henry. Leland then proposed that his longtime friend Charles Hargens, illustrator, would be just the man to create the paintings.

Dr. Henry was delighted, and negotiated with Hargens for the series to be painted. Leland sent to both of them a list of notable incidents in Lafayette's life—reviewing the troops with General Washington, being nursed back to health by a young woman after being wounded at the battle of the Brandywine, saving the life of Marie Antoinette, imprisonment in Olmutz— and so forth. Hargens set to work to finish seven 36-inch long paintings in about three months. Leland supplied all sorts of details, such as which of Lafayette's legs was wounded and which of his daughters had accompanied their mother on a visit to the prison in Czechoslovakia.

When the time came for the dedication, Waights Henry was suffering with the flu. Learning this, Leland put a slide show together entitled "Fifty Years of Backtracking Lafayette," and headed for Georgia. He gave his program at the college, gave it again at an assembly of service clubs, and twice at high schools, and attended all the ceremonies. "The Mayor of Le Puy and his wife were there," he said later," and my frail and fractured French nevairre got such a workout."

Dr. Henry had inspired another benefactor to build a new art center on the campus at LaGrange, and Joan gave her collection of Indian art, valued at the time at $50,000, to go in the center. The college, in turn, made her an honorary Doctor of Literature. She and Leland sent $5000 to endow a scholarship—the Josephine Altman Case Scholarship for excellence in art in the junior year, for someone showing promise in the arts field.

"My life is ideas," Leland wrote to Dr. and Mrs. Henry. "Ideas—those often squirming, sometimes sleepy, but never seen things that blend into what sometimes is called creativity. But ideas unattended are nothing. To be vital, they must be incubated and hatched." And, he said, Waight's creation of the Bicentennial event was an example of that exactly.

It was also an example of Leland's talent for building on the interest of another—Dr. Henry, and of casting about through his vast inventory of friends and acquaintances for the right supporting players in the drama - in this case Rene de Chambrun and Charles Hargens, and Wyoming sculptor Harry Jackson, whose foundry in Italy made the copy of the Lafayette statue for LaGrange. It was Leland who brought them all together.

The friendship between the Waights Henrys and the Leland Cases was a source of real happiness. Handwritten notes back and forth—Leland and Waights, Yellow Singing Bird and Mamie Lark—full of fun and the joy of language and the mind.

In 1979, Leland was made an honorary Doctor of Laws by LaGrange College. And Waights Henry's gratitude for Leland's efforts on behalf of La Grange took another form.

The thought of having a representation of James Earle Fraser's *The End of the Trail* masterpiece for the Friends of the Middle Border Museum was never far from Leland's consciousness. To his mind, Mitchell was the birthplace of the famous statue, and everything in him cried out that there should be a full-sized copy of it in a suitable place in the town.

The issue of the statue had been before Leland for almost 40 years. Why did no one in Mitchell respond enough to take this particular ball and run with it? At least part of the answer

229

came through Mark Rossi, a young sculptor in Tucson, son of Leland's old Westerner friend Paul Rossi. Paul had left the Gilcrease Institute in 1972 to pursue his own career as an artist and sculptor. When Leland asked Paul's advice about *The End of the Trail* he suggested his son Mark might help. Leland arranged for Mark to make an exploratory trip to Mitchell to acquaint himself with the situation first-hand, and to discover what might be possible in regard to *The End of the Trail*.

What Mark felt in talking with people around Mitchell was that time and the civil rights movement had changed many things in America and had brought new perspective to Indian and white in the Upper Missouri Valley, as it had to people all over the country. The Indian, Mark perceived, was not interested in the sense of defeat that *The End of the Trail* represented, and the white people of the community were not interested either. As a symbol for Mitchell, *The End of the Trail* just had no appeal.

What Leland felt about this report we may never know. But Dr. Waights Henry was aware of Leland's conviction to get a copy of the statue for Friends of the Middle Border. He also learned that Leland and Joan had an original Rembrandt print worth considerable money, that would look awfully grand in his new art center. Henry found the funds necessary to present an authentic 34-inch bronze copy of *The End of the Trail* to the Friends, and the Cases made a gift of their Rembrandt print to LaGrange College.

The *Mitchell Daily Republic* for December 3, 1980 carried a photo of *The End of the Trail* with the caption, "Home At Last". They printed the text of the inscription on the base of the statue: "This sculpture is a gift from LaGrange College, La Grange, Ga., honoring Drs. Leland D. and Josephine A. Case of Tucson, Arizona. Dr. Leland D. Case was founder of Friends of the Middle Border in 1939 and was a personal friend of the sculptor."

The piece stands now on a pedestal in the small but quite beautiful Leland D. and Josephine Case Dakota Art Gallery in the Friends of the Middle Border Museum, in the company of works of men and women most of whom are of South Dakota or the Upper Missouri Valley region—Harvey Dunn; Charles Hargens; Oscar Howe, a Sioux Indian artist who received some of his art training at Dakota Wesleyan; Ada Caldwell, who had been Harvey Dunn's first art teacher; Constance Garland Hayes, one of Hamlin Garland's two daughters; Gutzon Borglum; Frank Dorian; Anne Hyatt Huntington; and Marilyn Sunderman, Leland's niece. Out-of-doors and life-sized, in this day and age *The End of the Trail* might have been a divisive or at least embarrassing reminder of the past to the new mood of America. At 34 inches, it finds its place among the art of the region as a famous work by a renowned son of the Middle Border.

In the winter of 1977 the name of Don Sigler, former *Rotarian* staffer and longtime photographer, appears and marks an era in the affairs of the Westerners that ended only with his death a few weeks after that of Leland Case. Don had left *The Rotarian* to start his own business, a photo shop in Hannibal, Missouri. In truth, he was living on borrowed time. He had been born with a hole in his heart, and his doctor had not expected him to live to maturity. In 1977 he and his wife Lyda sold the business and moved to Tucson to give him a chance for a few more happy years.

Don responded to a siren song from Leland to become editor of the *Buckskin Bulletin*. He supplied for the *Bulletin* that element of continuity so important to a publication like this one.

231

1980—Westerners International board members meet with their current president, Jeff Dykes, second from right, Don Sigler, Editor of the Buckskin Bulletin, Jarvis Harriman, Executive Vice President, and Leland Case, Keeper of the Pitchfork

Don loved the Westerners. His constant contact with individuals and their corrals, with what they were doing and the things their corrals were involved in was invaluable grist for the *Bulletin's* mill, and for the health of the organization. It gave the paper a lot of life and intimacy.

During all the years of Don Sigler's editing the *Buckskin Bulletin*, Leland Case's name was listed along with his as comprising the editorial side of "the BB Bunch." Working together was like the fit of the legendary old shoe. Don would create an edition of the paper, have it set up in type, and send it to Leland. Leland would treat it with lavish doses from his purple ball-point pen and send it back. Don would grumble, but the changes would be made.

The End of the Trail Comes Home

The 84-year-old editorial consultant and his 74-year-old "protege" didn't miss much between them! They were both hard to work with, and it was hard for them to work together. Don grumbled a lot, but he had respected Leland ever since he had gone to work for him at *The Rotarian* in 1945.

Don was in and out of the hospital many times over this period, but with his wife by his side and work to do that kept his imagination and skills in high gear, he lived to be 76.

Ray Billington, as WI president in 1976, proposed that by the time The Westerners reached its 35th year there should be 100 corrals around the globe. I suspect that Leland and he hatched this idea together. Leland set to work on it and made it a goal for the executive committee and the board, and for anyone else he could reach with the concept. He kept a running tab on all the prospects for new corrals and on their progress. The anniversary year would be 1979. He wanted to be able to announce at the Westerner breakfast at the Western History Association meeting in San Diego that the target had been hit. It was, at the last moment, and he did.

Many jokes have been made about Leland's use of purple ink. Friends always mention it when reminiscing about him. I was so preoccupied with the subject matter as I delved through his files in the writing of this book that I do not have a good impression of how pervasive purple ink was through the years or when he might have started using it. But one item stuck in my mind—a letter Leland wrote late in 1977 to a Miss Susan Anderson in Elmsford, New York, in which he discusses his recent order for 50 purple-ink Softwriter #01401 pens. "But as I've reflected on your comment," he wrote, "about unused

233

markers drying out, it does occur to me that about twenty-five pens would run me through one year. So if it is feasible, please reduce my order to that number."

Some people have asked me how it was that the Cases could travel, acquire works of art, and do the things they did on a magazine editor's salary. Having discussed this with the executor of his estate, who had known Leland and Joan since the early sixties, and with Gordon Rollins and others, I feel quite comfortable in my answer.

First of all, Leland was paid a good salary at *The Rotarian*, once he was established, and also at *Together* and the Methodist Publishing House. And as a consultant, he knew his worth and received it.

Second, Leland and Joan knew how to save money. They spent it wisely. Often in the seventies some of us had lunch with him; it would mostly be at a Denny's, or Hardees—fast food or one step above fast food eateries. When the occasion called for it, we would plan a nice event at a private club, or at the university dining room. There was never a liquor bill, so dinners were not an expensive proposition. I saw the Cases several times having a quiet supper together at Piccadilly, a cafeteria well-known for its good, inexpensive food and Senior Citizen specials.

Third, the works of art usually came from browsing through second-hand shops or bookstores and picked up at a fraction of what later proved to be their worth. Some of the works were gifts to them.

Leland and Joan paid cash for things and did not pay interest to buy things "on time."

Not many of us these days know what frugal, well-thought-out living is and what it can save, or know the rewards of a lifetime of saving and investing wisely and persistently.

And then there was the land in Tucson, and how they leveraged it both to provide for their future and also for causes to which they were committed. It was land well-situated on a major arterial street, East Broadway, directly in the path of the city's growth. In the 1950s the price of raw land "out there" at 9900 East Broadway was in the range of $150 to $200 per acre. Its cash value increased dramatically over the next 36 years.

By the time of Leland's death, the land would sell for more like $30,000 per acre.

Over the years the Cases made several lifetime annuity arrangements from proceeds of sale of acreage, which secured an income for both of them; this income was relatively modest, as befitted their life-style. The gifts that they gave to Dakota Wesleyan University and Friends of the Middle Border, to Macalester College, to Black Hills State College, to La Grange College and to other charitable causes outweighed what they used for themselves. Altogether something like a million dollars was realized from their land.

The final 17.5 acres, upon which sits their Saguaro Homestead, will remain Joan's home until she dies. Leland arranged for it to pass into the hands of the City of Tucson; it will form the nucleus of a city park comprised of about 40 acres, the Leland D. and Josephine Case Park. The city paid what they could afford for this acreage and the Cases made the balance— about half of its market value—a gift to the city.

CHAPTER XI
The Trail's End

One of Leland's and Joan's friends was Katherine Pitkin, the widow of Walter the author, professor, and journalist, who had written for Leland at *The Rotarian* and had been a friend for many years. She commented to Leland on what she felt when she surveyed the Case Library. "You are among the few 'authentic' people I know," she said. "That is, you are as much a part of the smallest detail of your environment as anyone I can think of. You are, in a way, the Black Hills. Which means, of course, that you think about it, and grow with it and help to develop it. You are a part of that growth and development as if you were born in it and it in you."

Leland's friendships with people like Katherine went right on mellowing over the years. Lovick Pierce, who had hired him for the Methodist Publishing House, kept in touch through some hard times, especially when his wife died. Charles Ferguson corresponded with him frequently, as well as Charles Hargens; Ainslee Roseen of the old *Rotarian* gang; Herm Teeter, one of his key men at *Together*; Helen Webber, who as a volunteer worked hard on Friends of the Middle Border; and her daughter Sheila.

In May of 1980, while driving her own car, Joan had a severe auto accident. She suffered a broken arm and leg and other injuries. At her age, it was a traumatic experience that upset her severely. Leland moved his work from his adobe office into his bedroom to be near her. It was over six months before she was able to prepare dinner for Leland again, which she had usually done. He did not feel comfortable about working out in his office again until a year had passed.

236

The Westerners in Tucson, after their long use of the free space in the Southern Arizona Bank building on Campbell Avenue, had a series of searches and moves and searches again for donated headquarters. Leland would write a memorandum on the need, and would call upon the old Texan ballad for appropriate imagery—the boll weavil "jest a'lookin for a home." Leland thought in terms of eventually acquiring a building in which Westerners International would have headquarters, an ever-growing library, and perhaps collections of art and artifacts of the West.

He tried the idea on several friends in Tucson who owned attractive buildings, even their own homes. I know I shuddered at the thought, for all I could see was increased annual expense of maintenance, utilities, upkeep of the many sorts that we home owners know so well. Leland had bigger dreams for The Westerners than most of us, but what went through my mind was, "OK, you do it." If Leland had been 20 years younger, I would have said it aloud.

Leland fretted over the spreading use of the phrase "Native Americans." As he did with all incoming presidents at Dakota Wesleyan, he wrote to welcome Dr. James Beddow, in 1981, and shortly thereafter got into a dialogue with him about this phrase. "Native American" is unacceptable, Leland said, because it compounds error, twisting the meaning of "native" to please Indian militants who choose to take an adversarian stance; it violates an elemental principle of semantics: precision.

"Nearly a century ago," Leland wrote, "John Wesley Powell, the one-armed head of the Bureau of Ethnology of the Smithsonian Institution, suggested following a common practice used in linguistics of shortening 'American Indian' to this as a synonym: 'Amerind' or 'Amerindian'. As the (enclosed) Xeroxes from the Bibliographic Society of America show, scholars are more and more following the Powell lead. My hope in writing this is that DWU's Indian Program will side with the scholars. Some American Indians will bark about it, of course, but why shouldn't DWU be a leader in defence of precise English?"

In the 1980s Leland gave a great deal of attention to Friends of the Middle Border. It was as if he felt he had done what he had set himself to do for the Westerners, and now he could pay concentrated attention to his first love at Mitchell. He phoned and corresponded extensively with Bill Anderson, the executive director at that time, with members of the board of directors, and with Gordon Rollins.

As it had always been, money was the chief problem for Friends of the Middle Border. Leland recalled for Anderson his years of doing a whole host of things to support the activities he really believed in—the many jobs he took to pay his way through college and graduate school, for instance. "If I were you," Leland wrote, "I think I would try objectively to face up to the fact that I gotta solve the problem, myself. It may be easier to sit back and be a 'hired employee', but that assumes there's an 'employer' with ample funds available. FMB didn't start that way. It has earned its way."

But you had to be built like Leland Case to work that way, and although Bill may have come closer in interest and commitment than anyone since Jennewein, he was neither of them. He described for Leland how several institutions in the state like the Memorial Art Center at Brookings—created to house the paintings of Harvey Dunn—had programs like the things Leland longed to see at FMB—but, said Bill, "they have five full-time paid staff persons and a building one-third the size of ours to maintain."

In June, 1980, Black Hills State College conferred on Leland the Honorary Doctorate of Humane Letters. Joan was still suffering the effects of her many injuries from the accident, and Leland went by himself to Spearfish. He used the visit to see in detail what was happening with his library and to put in some time being sure the college president and the others were paying adequate attention to it.

And then he and his sister Carol attended the dedication of an historical marker just off the road into Hot Springs at Buffalo Gap, where Jedediah Smith is thought to have entered the Black Hills. The Jed Smith Corral of Westerners had worked on it with the state historical society, and here, years after Leland had first suggested it, was a tribute to Jed and his presence in the Hills.

We who worked together with Leland in the Executive Committee in Tucson had a bright thought one day: the time to express appreciation for Leland's work of establishing and developing The Westerners was then, while he was alive to enjoy it, rather than after he was gone.

We honored Leland in May of 1981 at "Ladies' Night" of the all-male Tucson Corral (which has since been integrated). We planned it as a surprise, with Joan's help, and surprise him we did. There were 300 people present. There were appropriate presentations from a number of corrals within driving distance; even Erl Ellis and his wife Scotty drove down from Denver to be there.

Leland Case was a man who gave thanks and a sense of appreciation readily and frequently. There were not many occasions, however, when we saw him taken by surprise and swept off his feet by something involving appreciation and thanks to him. Seldom did he put into words his reactions when something affected him deeply and moved him. Such a moment and such an expression came that night.

"Dazed, I finally groped my way to the mike," he wrote afterward to a host of friends. "But my mind flashed with recollections of co-founder Elmo Scott Watson whose grin once was likened by a poet to 'an acre of sunflowers.'" Elmo, with whom he had shared the infant growing pains of The Westerners. "And Ray Allen Billington who just weeks ago waved a friendly farewell from the High Divide." Ray, who had stood shoulder to shoulder with Leland in promoting the professional/amateur values of The Westerners and in the task of building it into a network rather than letting it drift as an amorphous flock of unrelated corrals. "These two and others," Leland wrote, "shared what Mark Twain called 'man's noblest delight'—discovering 'an intellectual nugget right under the dust of a field that many a brain plow has gone over before.' Ours was the vast potential of the Westerners."

Leland voiced his conviction that there should be an endowment fund for Friends of the Middle Border, and Dr. Lesta Turchen, professor of history at Dakota Wesleyan and current president of the board of the Friends, responded by telling him that she had started the legal machinery to create one. Leland offered to match up to $10,000 for the first $10,000 they would

240

F, Jack Anderson, president of the Old West Trail Foundation, presents the Westerner Award to Leland at Billings in 1983

raise for it, and before he was finished he had put many times that into it.

He began to look toward the year 1989, when Friends of the Middle Border would be 50 years old. He proposed creating a five-year plan to build up to it. He asked three men who had put effort into the organization as paid directors—Dean Nauman, Robert Pennington and Bill Anderson—if they would come to Tucson to think together about a suitable celebration and for the future. None of them was able to come. But what was in place for the fiftieth year was the endowment fund, which in the year 1989 topped $100,000. It was a start.

George Bittner, the young owner-operator of a funeral home in Mitchell, became president of Friends of the Middle Border in 1985. He did not know Leland Case, but Leland telephoned him to congratulate him, and to talk about FMB with him. They hit it off. After that Leland phoned him almost every Sunday to

241

see how things were going and to comment on what was happening.

As the '80s—and his own 80s—wore on, Leland's mind stayed as active as ever. His turn came around at the Tucson Literary Club, to present a paper, and he put together the story of how he won over the four key critics of Rotary International back in the thirties. He called it "Revamping an Image." It displayed the same easy, masterful writing style he had always used.

In 1983 he was honored with the Westerner Award, given by the Old West Trail Foundation in Rapid City, an organization dedicated to encouraging travel and tourism in the Dakotas, Wyoming, Montana and Nebraska. They cited him as founder of Friends of the Middle Border and then co-founder of Westerners International, his library at Black Hills State College, his wife's Indian art collection at LaGrange College, and "a sincere zeal for making better known the authentic history of America's frontier." The award was given to him at their annual banquet, which on this occasion was held in Billings, Montana. Leland travelled there by himself, and landed at the Billings airport.

His sister Carol had made up her mind to surprise him and join him at the banquet. She took a tedious bus ride from Hot Springs to get there and was met by their mutual friend Mary Morsanny of the Never Sweat Ranch. Leland got off the plane, and Carol threw her arms around him. It was like old times. After the banquet the three of them, Carol and Leland and Mary, took a tour of the Custer Battlefield.

Leland built up several files entitled "Memoirs" in the '80s, as if in preparation for writing his own. They contained clippings on all manner of things he had witnessed or knew about over the years—politics, personalities, world trends, journalism, collections of Black Hills tales, Preacher Smith's last sermon, Custer's dispatches to his wife, to name but a few.

His mind kept reaching out to new facets of history. He wrote to the Homestake Mining Company to find out what was the practical basis of the use of the myth, in the prospecting days in the Black Hills, of "the golden fleece". He learned that the small, individual placer mine operations literally used in the sluice water a hunk of sheeps' fleece that would catch gold dust.

Willmon White, editor of *The Rotarian,* and his associate editor Jo Nugent, asked Leland if he could join the other former editors of the magazine in a salute to its 75th anniversary in 1986. They were including brief comments from Chesley Perry, its first editor, now deceased, on how the magazine began, and they wanted a contribution from Leland and one from Karl Krueger. Leland far exceeded the space requirements they assigned him, but what he wrote was fascinating, and they included much of it. It was lively vintage Case, as up-to-date as his prose had been 60 years ago. He ended it with a description of how he got Albert Einstein to write for the magazine. "I recall no other feature that generated more personal satisfaction for me," the article concluded. "I had persuaded Albert Einstein, the exponent of Relativity, not to say Nein, but Jah! I could add Q.E.D.—but of course, in a very relative sort of way."

As if the Black Hills were reluctant to let him go, an attempt was made, a year before his death, by a Rapid City man to revive *Lee's Official Guidebook.* He had been struck by all

Friends of the Middle Border museum grounds include (left to right) the Farwell church, the Sheldon schoolhouse, and the Beckwith home (courtesy of Friends of the Middle Border)

that Leland had poured into the little book. A number of consultations followed in which Leland was energetic and inspiring to the younger man but not interested personally in tackling the project again.

Leland, though in his office and around the house, was tired-tired-tired. In the fall, with so little energy, he sought medical help and his doctors discovered cancer. They soon found that it was throughout his body. By mid-September he was in bed most of the time. George Bittner and his wife came down from Mitchell to see him Friends around Tucson paid calls at the house. My wife and I went to see him, and found that his mind came and went—although when it was with us, it was clear. By mid-December he was in a coma for a few days, and he died on December 16, right there in his own Saguaro Homestead.

244

A funeral service was held at St. Paul's United Methodist Church. Joan was there, supported by her friends, and those of us who had carried the ball with Leland in The Westerners. Don Sigler got out of his bed to be at that service. It seemed to signal to Don the final moments of the ball game, for six weeks later—as his wife Lyda had predicted—he followed Leland.

At the church Leland and Joan attended originally in Tucson, Catalina United Methodist, there is a pleasant little walled garden, with wrought iron gates, grass, an olive tree and rose bushes, and a fountain of the Spanish Colonial style that is the Southwest. There Leland's ashes nourish the ground, along with others, and there is a small bronze plaque for each person. It is a sun-drenched, friendly place, and from the park across the street you can hear children playing. At the entrance is a sign embodying that imaginative use of our growing, changing language that he loved and revelled in—

"A Place Sacred To The Memory
of Those Whose Cremains Are Here"

EPILOGUE

What do you say about this man who lived for the first 86 years of this century? a century of great change, of great growth, of tremendous upheaval, of magnificent opportunity?

First of all, he rode with it. He tasted it. He relished it.

Second, in many ways he understood it.

And third, perhaps as only a few of his contemporaries did, he strove to direct it.

He thought out and applied to his century the basic values and convictions that he had inherited and that he felt were fundamental to any time and place. And then, choosing to spend his 30 most productive years at this task, he devoted his professional career to influencing the age he lived in.

With *The Rotarian*, he accepted using a magazine to feed and mold the thinking of a group of people who, it could be argued, are as influential, from grass roots to summit of power, as any group of people in the world. For the Methodist Church, his spiritual heritage, he assayed to interpret through *Together* their basic message for men, women and children living in the modern world and coping with it.

In his avocation he did the same. The things he worked at—Friends of the Middle Border, The Westerners, the Jedediah Smith Society, the Archives and History Commission of the Methodist Church, the Deadwood United Methodist Historical Society, the Leland Case Library for Western Historical Studies—all were guideposts to the future. They all celebrate the qualities of the human spirit and the human experience that guarantee the future. And how he worked at them! "Look to the rock from whence you were hewn." Vigorous, whole-hearted, optimistic, almost never preachey, always exuberant.

Will Leland Case be forgotten?

Undoubtedly his name—not widely known now—will mean less and less to anyone as time goes by.

The things he created—left behind, if you will—that he built with his mind and his vision, with his heart and his vast energy, and with his genius for promotion, are growing and feeding hundreds and thousands of people—today, even as you read these pages:

Friends of the Middle Border is steadily if slowly growing. Over 10,000 people visited it in its five-month season in 1994. A thousand school children took guided tours through its exhibits and got a picture of life in pioneer South Dakota and the persistence, faith and imagination it took to carve a life out of that rolling country.

The use of the many collections for research, both by Dakota Wesleyan students and others in the community, is growing steadily. Officials of the city of Mitchell and of Davison County, as well as the general public, look to FMB for historical reference. Social events—period fashion shows at the charming Beckwith home, reunions of graduates of the Sheldon Township schoolhouse, religious services in the Farwell church—regularly take place on the grounds. The American Indian gallery and the Case art gallery are used by both Dakota Wesleyan and the University of South Dakota.

The future of FMB is the more secure because of a good-sized Case trust that will provide income when Joan Case no longer needs its support.

The Westerners is a steady influence for fresh insight and

understanding into the development of our country and, like Mrs. Miniver's rearview mirror, is a link between our past, our present and our future. Since Leland's death in 1986 there have been thirteen new corrals chartered—in Texas, Colorado, Nebraska, Oklahoma, Utah, Arizona, and in Belgium, England and no less than five in Czechoslovakia. The total is now 131. The headquarters of Westerners International is now at the National Cowboy Hall of Fame & Western Heritage Center in Oklahoma City where it has a higher visibility than ever.

Deadwood now has legalized gambling, as that small picturesque community struggles with 1990s economic needs, but the Deadwood United Methodist Historical Society's Preacher Smith Heritage Center is a steady—and well visited—reminder of what it takes to build a community and a civilization.

LaGrange College has the Leland and Josephine Case Indian Arts collection on permanent display, and the Charles Hargens paintings of Lafayette.

The Jedediah Smith Society functions steadily from its base in Stockton.

The Leland D. Case Library for Western Historical Studies now contains over 18,000 items. Five hundred and fifty-five people made use of the collections between October 1992 and September 1993; 2,446 new items were acquired, plus 37 boxes of material not yet unpacked or sorted; 203 new patrons were registered, for a total of 1,974; 998 hours of work-study and volunteer time were put into the library.

Dr. David Miller of the History Department at Black Hills State University (it became a university in 1989) reports that the Case library has been a key resource for the school to offer courses in Black Hills History, Wyoming history, specialized classes for teachers, workshops on contemporary regional mining issues, local history for social studies teachers, a historiography course (methods classes for historians), specialized library and original source research training for history majors going into graduate work, and a master's degree in tourism with emphasis on history.

The collections the library contains have been magnets that have drawn others. The files of Arrow, Inc., a private group headquartered in Washington D.C. promoting better relations between Indians and non-Indians, are now at the Case library, along with many books and artifacts from them as well as funds to maintain the materials; also acquired have been the files of the Bald Mountain Mining Company, second only to the Homestake Mine in Black Hills history; and dozens of other similar collections. The Leland Case Library is materially affecting the standard and scope of education and research in Leland's Black Hills.

Joan Case can look out over their cactused acres, and the sun comes in through the D'Ascenzo stained glass panel into their living room. The creatures of the desert, even the diamond-back rattlesnakes that Fritz used to sniff out, enjoy the acres with her.

And in the future, the city of Tucson, by an arrangement Leland set up before he died, will develop the Leland D. and Josephine A. Case Park on their land, for future desert dwellers to enjoy.

Leland built well, provided well, and the things he started grow year by year, though his own footsteps can be seen no more.

Bibliography

My basic source of material for this biography has been the collection of Leland Case's papers which were made available to me by the executor of his estate, Lyle Halvorson of Tucson. Comprising over a hundred file boxes, they were rich with handwritten and typed notes going back over his life, the earliest being about the age of thirteen. They have now gone to the archives of Friends of the Middle Border, in Mitchell, South Dakota.

Francis Case: A Political Biography, by Richard Chenoweth, University of Nebraska (doctoral dissertation 1977), Lincoln

Fall River County Pioneer History, Fall River County Historical Society, Hot Springs, 1976

Interview with Leland D. Case, by Robert G. Webb, Professor of History at Northern State College, Aberdeen, at Mitchell, April 23, 1972

New Hampshire to Minnesota—Memoirs of Samuel Higbee Grannis 1839-1933 Edited by Leland D. Case and Edith E. H. Grannis, published by Edith Emily Higbee Grannis, Tucson, 1962

Back to the Black Hills, by Leland D. Case, illustrated by Bates Littlehales, National Geographic, National Geographic Society, Washington, D.C., Volume CX Number Four, October 1956

The Black Hills, edited by Roderick Peattie, Vanguard Press, Inc, New York 1952

The Black Hills Historian, Volume I Number 1, February 1977, Black Hills State University, Spearfish

A Dakota Boyhood by James Earle Fraser, American Heritage, December 1968

End of the Trail by Adele Renee Malott, Editor, Friendly Exchange, March 1981

End of the Trail—Odyssey of a Statue by Dean Krakel, University of Oklahoma Press, Norman, 1973

Most Famoun Unknown Statue by Aline B. Leuchheim, condensed from The New York Times Magazine, Reader's Digest, September 1951

Friends of the Middle Border Museum of Pioneer Life, Mitchell, South Dakota by Mildred Soladay, Fulton, 1977

James Truslow Adams by Allan Nevins, University of Illinois Press, Urbana-Champaign, 1973

Lee's Official Guidebook to the Black Hills and the Badlands, Black Hills and Badlands Association, Sturgis, 1949

Preacher Smith, Martyr by Leland D. Case, Preacher Smith Memorial

Association, Deadwood, reprinted 1976

Middle Border Bulletin, Friends of the Middle Border, Mitchell, various issues

Phreno Cosmian, Dakota Wesleyan University, Mitchell, various isues

Fifty Years of Rotary, Rotary International, Chicago, 1955

My Road to Rotary, Paul Harris, A. Croch & Sons, Chicago, 1948

Rotary Mosaic by Harold T. Thomas, Rotary Clubs of New Zealand, 1974

Seventy-five Years of Rotary, Rotary International, Chicago, 1980

The First Rotarian by James P. Walsh, Scan Books, London, 1979

The Rotarian Reader—75 Year Anthology, Rotary International, Chicago, 1986

This Rotarian Age by Paul Harris, Rotary International, Chicago, 1935

The World of Rotary, Rotary International, Chicago

University of Chicago Study of the Rotary Club of Chicago

The Rotarian, Rotary International, Evanston, bound volumes 1911-present

Brand Book I, Tucson Corral of The Westerners, Tucson 1967

Buckskin Bulletin, 1960-present, Westerners Foundation, Stockton and Westerners International, Tucson and Oklahoma City

The Westerners: Twenty-five Years of Riding the Range by Leland D. Case, *Western Historical Quarterly*, Vol.I No.1, January 1970, Western History Association, Albuquerque

Don Russell article in *The Western Historical Quarterly*, July 1973, Western History Association, Albuquerque

History of The Westerners by J.E. Reynolds, reprinted 1957 from The Los Angeles Corral Brand Book #7, Los Angeles

The Westerners Brand Book, Chicago Corral of The Westerners, various editions, Chicago

The Westerners by Don Russell, *Guns Magazine*, May 1971

The Westerners, by Steward Edward White, Grosset & Dunlap, New York, 1901

Augustana College Center for Western Studies, Sioux Falls

Arizona Historical Society, Tucson, Michael F. Weber, Executive Director, Bruce Dinges, Director of Publicationa, Adelaide Elm, former Archivist, Margaret Bret Harte, Librarian

Black Hills Regional United Methodist Historical Society, The Rev. Dwayne Knight and Mrs. Marjorie Pontius

Daily Christian Advocate (record of the proceedings of the General Conference of the Methodist Church 1952-65) Garrett Theological Seminary Library, Evanston

Dakota Wesleyan University, Mitchell, Dr. James Bedow, President, Linda Ritter, Librarian

252

Drew University Library, Madison, Dr. Kenneth Rowe, Librarian
Friends of the Middle Border Museum, Mitchell, Hazel Jordan, Director
LaGrange College, LaGrange, Walter Y. Murphy, President, and John
    Lawrence, Chairman of the Art Department
Leland D. Case Library for Western Historical Studies, Black Hills State
    University, Spearfish, Dr. Edwin Erickson, Librarian, Dora Jones, Curator
Lutheran Information Service of the Evangelical Lutheran Church in America,
    Chicago
Macalester College, St. Paul, Robert Gavin, President
Medill School of Journalism of Northwestern University, Evanston
Methodist Infoserve, Nashville
Middle Border Bulletin various editions, Friends of the Middle Border,
    Mitchell
The papers of Don Russell, Elmo Scott Watson and The Westerners,
    Newberry Library, Chicago
Phreno Cosmian various editions, Dakota Wesleyan University, Mitchell
South Dakota Department of Tourism, Pierre
South Dakota State Historical Society, Pierre, Julius R. Fisher, Executive
    Director
Archives of the United Methodist Conference Center, Mitchell
Tucson-Pima Public Library, Tucson, Elizabeth Gonzales, Director
United Methodist Publishing House, Nashville, Robert K. Feaster, President,
    and Roslyn Lewis
University of Arizona Library, and Special Collections, Tucson
University of the Pacific, Stockton, Dr. Bill Atchley, President, Cynthia
    Stevenson, Archivist

Acknowledgments

My wife and I have known Leland and Joan Case since 1973. We see Mrs. Case occasionally in her home in Tucson.

We were fortunate to be able to visit at length with Leland's sister, Caroline Case Goddard, in her home in Hot Springs, South Dakota, and with his youngest sister, Esther Case Sunderman, in LeSeuer, Minnesota. We have also gotten to know his niece, Lois Wilson Saunders and her husband Philip, in Rapid City, South Dakota. By correspondence and telephone we have become friends with Lois's sister Dorothy Wilson Fowler, her brother, Allen Wilson, and Esther's daughter Marilyn Sunderman. Through Marilyn's kindness we have reproduced her portrait of her uncle which now hangs in the Case Dakota Art Gallery of Friends of the Middle Border. I also visited with Leland's cousin Mrs. Harrison Schmitt, mother of the astronaut-senator-geologist, in her home in Silver City, New Mexico, and consulted the Cases' attorney Richard Duffield.

The people I have called upon, visited, telephoned, consulted in this work are many. Among them are Mrs. Eugene Norman and Mrs. Norval Langworthy, friends of Mrs. Case; Miss May Aaberg, of Washington, D.C.; Harold Cooley (since deceased), Karl and Dorothy Krueger (Karl died this year); Willmon White, Jo Nugent, Paige Carlin and Cathy Longston in their Rotary International offices; Anthony J. Tolbert who was Leland's assistant at *Together*; Dean Nauman of Littleton, Colorado; Gordon and Elsie Rollins, George Bittner, Mrs. Catherine Morgan, Mrs. Mildred Soladay, Jon Ehrhardt, and Karl Koch all of Mitchell, South Dakota; Mrs. Ellen Blanchard Schroeder; Charles W. Hargens; and Dr. David Miller, at Black Hills State University.

About the Methodist Church—Donald Baker, the Rev. Stan Brown, Dr. Ernest R.Case, Dr. Henry Hottman, Dr. Frederick E. Maser, Dr. Howard Mumma, and Dr. Ewing T. Wayland.

Westerners Otis Chidester, Fred Egloff, Alvin Krieg, Melville Williams, Norman Parker, Watson Parker, Will K. Brown, Harry Anderson, L. Boyd Finch, Bernard Fontana, Earl McCoy, George Godfry, John Marshall, Frederick A. Meyer, Dan Lapinsky, James Shebl, Marshall Truax, Bob Lee, John Porter Bloom, Don Reeves, James E. Griffith, Michael Harrison, Pat Henry, Charles W. Hill, Harwood Hinton, Dean Krakel, David Laird, Mark Rossi, Greg Franzwa and William Hawes Smith.

And John Mack Carter, Bart McDowell, Larry Raymer, Mrs. Don Sigler, Dawn Cromwell, Paul Dyck, John Gilcrease, A. Tracy Row, Dr. Arthur Raymond, Kenneth R. Philp, and Ed Tanner.

Special thanks for the unfailing help of the Info Line of the Tucson Pima Library.

On behalf of Westerners International and me, much thanks to those who

254

have contributed money to make this book possible - The Leland Case Estate, Lyle Halvorson, Executor, and Caroline Case Goddard, Lois and Phil Saunders, Allen Wilson, Kathryn Harriman, Melville C. Williams, Walter and Isabel Fathauer, Boyd and Polly Finch, Mary Morsanny, Barbara and Jerry von Teuber, Gordon and Elsie Rollins, Fred Egloff, Marc T. Campbell Sr., Hermann K. Bleibtreu, Will K. Brown, Arthur Hotson, Mrs. Carl Sundstrom, David Laird, Norman Flanders, Robert K. Johnson (since deceased), Anthony J. Tolbert, Watson Parker, Donald Shropshire, Lora Crouch, John G. Streeter, The United Methodist Publishing House, and the Arthur H. Clark Company.

And for financial help from the following Westerner units—Kansas City Posse, Jedediah Smith Corral, Dallas Corral, Prescott Corral, Llano Estacado Corral, Sacramento Corral, Kaw Valley Corral, Adobe Corral, Dakota Midland Corral, Santa Catalina Corral, Kansas Corral, Potomac Corral, San Francisco Corral, Yellowstone Corral, Yuma Crossing Corral, Rancho del Norte Corral.

Many thanks to David Dary, and Paul and Florence Rossi, for their constant help, and for Paul's drawing of Leland, the porcupine, the rifle and the rock.

To the Hon. George McGovern for his introduction.

A heartfelt salute to five Westerners who have gone beyond since helping with this work - Donald Bufkin, Bob Johnson, Peyton Reavis, Leland Sonnichsen, and Dan Thrapp.

To Bob Blackburn and Mary Ellen Meredith of Oklahoma City and Westerners International for shepherding this work through the publishing process, to Bruce Dinges, and to Omega Clay, jacket designer.

And to Wallace Clayton, Publisher-Editor of the Tombstone Epitaph for his invaluable support—and to Nancy Dole Harriman, my wife.

Index

A

Aaberg, May 59, 60, 71, 81, 90, 159, 183, 186
Aberdeen, SD 26
Acacia Fraternity 29
D'Ascenzo 47, 250
Adams, James Truslow 78, 83, 86, 88, 99, 107, 110, 116
— The American Dream 83, 86, 116
— Epic of America 88
Adams, Jane 29
Adams, Kay (Mrs.James Truslow Adams) 83
Aero Club de France 34
Albright, John 208
Albuquerque, NM 43
Alderson, William 221
Allen, Ira 156(photo)
Altman, Dr.Frank DeGraff (father-in-law) 41
Altman, Josephine (see also Case, Josephine Altman and Case, Joan) 40, 41, 42
Altman, Josephine Smith (mother in law) 50, 68
American Academy of Arts and Letters 78, 83, 107
American Association of State and Local History 221
American Dream, The (see also James Truslow Adams) 83, 86
American Mountain Series, Vanguard Press 119
American Revolution 19
American Revolution Bicentennial 222
Anderson, Bill 238, 241
Anderson, Clinton Presba 43, 46, 53, 54, 72, 75, 78, 96, 108, 128, 149, 152
Anderson, F. Jack 241(photo)
Anderson, Miss Susan 233
Anglo-French Press Association 32
Apollo XVII 220
Appleseed, Johnny 162
Arizona Highways 138
Arizona Historical Society 201, 214
Arminian Magazine 166
Arminius, Jacob 166

Armour Company 56
Army Air Corps 90
Around the Copy Desk 68, 70, 110, 141
Arrow, Inc. 250
Asbury, Francis 185
Associated Church Press 145
Association of Methodist Historical Societies, see Methodist Historical Societies, Association of 175-176
Atchison, KS 41
Atherton, Warren 191
Atlantic 55
Augustana College, Center for Western Studies 116, 212

B

Baccarat glass 36
Badger Hole, The 125
Baker, Frank E. 167(photo)
Baker, Josephine 32
Bald Mountain Mining Company 250
Bancroft Library, University of California at Berkeley 161, 218
Barnes, Ralph 34
Baskette, Floyd 145, 182
Bastian, George C. 39, 41, 48
— *Editing the Day's News* 39 - see *Editing the Day's News*
— *Around the Copy Desk* 68, 70, 110, 141
— Mrs. Bastian 44, 51, 52
Battle Mountain Sanitarium 17
Bax, L.Drew 129
Bear Butte 7, 8, 10, 16, 27, 105, 123
Beddow, Dr.James 237
Bede, The Venerable 222
Beef Trust Girls 58
Belle Fourche, SD 27, 109, 146
Beloit College 93
Bemis, Ed 147
Bennett-Clarkson Hospital, formerly Deaconess Hospital, Rapid City SD 18
Bernays, Edward L. 121-123
Berring, Henry (see also Dakota Wesleyan University Black Hills College gates) 108
Berry, E.Y. 186, 216

257

Index

Index

Index

Index

Index

Index

Index

Index

Index

Index

Index

Index

Index

270

Index

Index

Index

B CAS 79-96

Harriman

THE MAN FROM THE HILLS: A BIOGRAPHY OF
LELAND D. CASE

DATE DUE
